CLASSIC PAINTING

THIS VOLUME, EDITED
BY ANDRÉ GLOECKNER,
WAS FIRST PUBLISHED
IN NINETEEN HUNDRED
AND FIFTY-ONE BY THE
HYPÉRION PRESS, PARIS.
PRINTING OF THE TEXT,
ENGRAVINGS AND COLOR-
PLATES BY IMPRIMERIE
CRÉTÉ, CORBEIL, FRANCE.

HISTORY OF

CLASSIC PAINTING

Published under the supervision of

GERMAIN BAZIN

Curator of the Museum of the Louvre,
Professor at the École du Louvre.

Translated from the French by
ROSAMUND FROST

Text, research, biographies, bibliographies by
MARC LOGÉ, ANDRÉ LECLERC, M. DE GESNE,
FREDERICK MOSS, S. BÉGUIN.

Published by
THE HYPÉRION PRESS, NEW YORK - PARIS - LONDON

Distributed by
THE MACMILLAN COMPANY NEW YORK

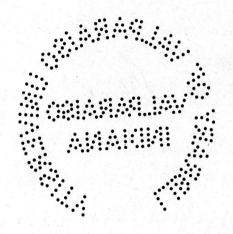

CONTENTS

In small compass, this volume conceived by André Gloeckner for Hyperion Press presents a vast anthology of Western painting. [You] will find here a magnificent succession of colorplates, brief texts wh[ich] codify the great schools of art and, in the last analysis, an art diction[ary]. All are part of a book planned by its editor to help those who wis[h to] know more about the history of painting.

The reproductions are accorded a primary place and the text orie[nts] itself accordingly. Diverse chapters succeed one another, some wri[tten] in England, others in France. It was my job to co-ordinate th[ese] viewpoints, shaping out of them an organic unity, revising the ch[oice] of illustrations and documentation.

This is the classic test of Western painting carried to its ultim[ate] extension, attaining even the American continent as it unrolls its cou[rse]. It is the moving colloquy of the artist with nature, pursued in her se[cret] ways, courted for her appearances, confided in by the man of aspiratio[n,] the tormented of heart; or else victim of the violating artist, yield[ing] herself to him. For it is by assault that the artist relieves himself [of] his agonies and sufferings. On the other hand, nature shapes her[self] to meet his speculations halfway. But whether in the artist's soul [or] outside of it, eternally she is there. And like a play, the Western wo[rld] watches the spectacle, as absorbed as if witnessing the birth of the wor[ld.]

Only modern man, in his audacity, could break this conspiracy a[nd] conceive of the work of art as an autonomous creation endowed with [its] own traits, destined to disseminate messages beyond the reach of [our] ordinary senses. Does the future hold for us a sublime "twilight of [re]presentation" as I have already predicted? Or, carried away by the co[m]pelling arguments of Gaston Diehl, should we recognize the dawn of [a] new age?

GERMAIN BAZIN

ORIGINS

CHRISTIAN ART

BYZANTINE ART.—4th century. Painted surface of a quadrangular casket (detail). Baltimore, Henry Walters Collection.

Hardly perceptible is the transition from ancient to medieval esthetics; in its early works Byzantine art continues to evoke Alexandrian grace.

WITH the advent of Christianity, a new, art emerged slowly from that of antiquity. It was at first essentially a funerary art, confined to the humble paintings which decorated the catacombs, or underground cemeteries, in particular those of Rome. Obeying spiritual preoccupations and also perhaps an elementary caution imposed upon them by the political circumstances of the time, the artists resorted to symbolical and allegorical forms to express the great truths of the new faith. Thus, to personify the immortal soul, they created the lovely figure of a young girl praying near the grave. Likewise, a fish often represented Christ, and a dove the soul of the faithful. Although far from equalling in quality even the inferior decorations of Pompeii, these simple paintings succeeded in expressing a high moral teaching.

Among the finest of these primitive frescoes are those of the catacombs. The style of these obscure Christian artists, who had doubtless learned their craft from pagan masters, bore a strong resemblance to the works of secular painters of the same period; the small Psyches and winged cherubs of Alexandrian art were often used to express the tribulation of the Christian's soul.

However, Christian art was soon to abandon the obscurity to which Roman intolerance had condemned it. At the beginning of the 4th century, the Emperor Constantine recognized Christianity as the official religion and thus modified the destinies of art, and even of society in general.

When the new faith was openly preached in magnificent basilicas, gorgeous decorations took the place of the humble paintings of yore. These, while laying considerable stress on historical interest, also expressed the ideal of grandeur and of domination which now animated the Christian

CHRISTIAN ART.—End of the 2nd century. Orante. Rome, Catacomb of Priscilla.—*Early Christian art borrows from ancient art its forms and, at time even its motifs, of which it changes only the meaning.*

faith promoted to the role of universal power. The early artists of Byzantium, when depicting Christ or the Virgin, sought to inspire themselve when possible from so-called authentic documents. Christ was no longe represented (as in the catacombs) as a clean-shaven Roman citizen, clad i a toga; he now appeared in all the magnificence of an Oriental monarcl seated on a splendid throne surrounded by a court of angels. The Virgir who formerly recalled a demure Roman matron, was clad in a Syrian car in early Byzantine art.

Thus, during the 4th century, the Christian artists who had acces to the basilicas created a new style. Unfortunately, few of their painting have been preserved. We can, however, form some idea of their ar thanks to the frescoes and mosaics which have defied the ravages of tim and which were their favorite modes of expression.

LATIN MANUSCRIPT.—Portrait of Charlemagne. Paris, Bibliothèque Natio-ale. *This miniature, left unfinished, reveals all the supple qualities of Carlo-vingian design.*

BYZANTINE ART

Byzantine art is distinctly Asiatic in the gorgeousness of its coloring and its preference for the magnificence of the materials employed rather than elegance and beauty of form. Byzantine churches were considered

BYZANTINE ART.—4th century. Painted surface of a quadrangular casket (detail). Baltimore, Henry Walters Collection.

finished only when they had receive their interior and exterior polychrom decorations. Thus mosaic became th favorite means of ornamentation Byzantine art, and gradually impose its style upon a school of painting from which all effects in relief were banne

The high dignitaries of the Church ha early realized how art could serve the to propagate the new faith. The therefore encouraged the artists of th time to create images which replaced so to speak, the Holy Book for th ignorant mass of the people. Soo these images came to play an activ part in the cult itself. Thus icons mad their appearance, being easy to interpre and to understand. It has been sai very justly that the invention of Chris tian iconography was the truly origina achievement of Byzantine art. Later under the influence of European art, the figures of the icons were to ac quire more life ; we owe the original models of early Christianity to th Orient.

Byzantine art, being religious in inspiration and Asiatic and Greek in sources, required images to express itself. Those it created were flat and purposely deprived of naturalism, the better to express the world beyond This iconography came near to disappearing in the 8th century, when sev eral emperors, in their zeal to reform both Church and State, denounced and banned all holy images as relics of a pagan past. The quarrel of the icon oclasts lasted from 726 to 742 A.D., and ended in the victory of the image-makers. This dispute seems even to have stimulated the ardor of religious painters for, far from submitting to the threats of the iconoclasts they pursued their work undaunted, while a parallel school of more inde pendent artists sought inspiration in antique models.

Soon the symbolical themes of early Christian art were replaced by Gospel scenes. The pictorial version of the story of Christ and the Virgin first appeared in the 4th and 5th centuries. Without doubt Byzantine iconography fixed the types and attitudes of the personages represented in these early works, it was to be the task of a more naturalistic art, that of the monks of Cappadocia and Asia Minor, to interpret successfully the moving poetry and pathos of the episodes depicted.

Bible of Charles the Bald. Tours, between 846 and 851.—Abbé Vivien presenting a Bible to Charles the Bald surrounded by his officers. Paris, Bibliothèque Nationale.

The circular arrangement of the figures around the throne attests to the disappearance of the ancient sense of perspective.

APOCALYPSE OF SAINT-SEVER.—11th century. The Triumph of the Lamb
Paris, Bibliothèque Nationale.

*In the 8th century, a Spanish monk, Beatus, composed a commentary on the
Apocalypse which was often illustrated in Catalonia and in France. The
most beautiful copy is the one illuminated between 1028 and 1072 at the abbey
of Saint-Sever in the Landes, under the abbacy of Gregory, by the miniaturist
Stephanus Garcia, who was undoubtedly a Spaniard. The figures standing
out against a uniform background evoke the fresco technique, and the "cloisonné"
aspect of the tones makes one think of enamel-work or stained-glass windows;
the extraordinary brilliance of the colors, with vermillion red and saffron
yellow dominant, will be found in Catalonia in painting on panels and in
frescoes until the following century. The manuscript of Beatus inspired
one of the first great works of Romanesque sculpture, the portal of
Moissac.*

A little later, miniatures by more or less skilful artists made known to all
Christendom the decorative style of the Byzantine frescoes and monumental
mosaics. The Benedictine monks, in particular, were indefatigable in
painting these small images, a series of which was often necessary to reproduce the large mural which served as model. Thus it came to pass that
monasteries soon possessed real art schools, the source of which could be
traced to the East.

Si come abraham en maine sen fill pur sacrefier.

Si come ille uiout sacrefier.

SALTER OF INGEBURGE OF DENMARK, Queen of France (before 1236).—
braham departs for the sacrifice. Sacrifice of Isaac. Chantilly, Musée
Condé.

*his work of transition shows the efforts of the artist to free himself from the
conventions of Romanesque art.*

ROMANESQUE ART

During several centuries, the Western world was plunged in wild cha
and confusion hardly propitious to the development of art. Roman ci
lization was overthrown by barbarian invasions, and from Constantine
the Romanesque period, humanity seems to have wantonly dissipated
heritage instead of seeking to increase or even preserve it. The Germ
invaders practised only decorative arts in keeping with their nomac
habits. Once settled and converted to Christianity, they succumbed to t
influence of the West and built or enriched many basilicas, such as th
of Saint Martin de Tours, in Merovingian Gaul. Most of these edifices we
but poor imitations of the vigorous Roman conceptions. In paintin
the decadence was still more evident.

It was only at the end of the 8th century and the beginning of the 9
that Charlemagne, seeking to reconstruct an immense empire, resolved
give new impetus to art. He even solicited the co-operation of forei
artists, some of whom, according to tradition, came from overseas. /
Aix-la-Chapelle (called "the New Rome" by the Emperor's contemporarie
palaces like Ingelheim were embellished with fine decorations in whi
the influence of antiquity was very noticeable, the exploits of Cyrus, tl
conquests of Alexander, the lives of Theodosius and of Constantine a
being represented. To-day, only a few manuscripts illustrated by mini
turists of the Carlovingian epoch give us an idea of painting in the 7th ar
9th centuries. Some are, however, of capital importance, such as the Eva
geliaire, or book containing the Gospels for each mass, offered to Charles tl
Bold by the monks of Saint Martin de Tours, and the Bible of Saint Pa
Outside the Walls at Rome, which was decorated by the French mon
Ingobert.

In the confusion and wars following Charlemagne's death, art wou
have suffered an almost total eclipse had it not been for the refuge offere
it by the monasteries which abounded in Gaul. There, in the quiet of tl
cloisters, many art schools were founded. Monks who were also painter
goldsmiths and architects were free to pursue their artistic vocations undi
turbed by the vicissitudes of turbulent times.

The pagan Saracen, Hungarian and especially Norman invaders who no
overran the land, burnt down many religious edifices. A chronicler of tl
time says that "at that epoch all the churches of Gaul were burnt dow
with the exception of those situated in a few fortified cities." Good wa

SCHOOL OF PARIS, about 1360-1364.—Portrait of King John the Good (?).
Paris, Musée du Louvre.

This work is the oldest European portrait painting; it is supposed to have been part of a group in which figured also the portraits of Edward III of England, Charles IV, Emperor of Germany, and Charles V, then Duke of Normandy.

[15]

PARISIAN SCHOOL, about 1373-1378.—Altar-frontal of Narbonne. Paintin on silk. Right section: Series of scenes from the life of Christ. Pari Musée du Louvre.

At the time of Charles V, painting and miniature work tend to reduce to pu graphism, which emphasizes the nervousness of the Gothic line.

however, to spring out of this destruction; for after the fall of the Carlovin gian dynasty, and at the accession to power of the Capetians, the signs of a indisputable artistic renascence appeared. Around 1003, says the chron icler Raoul Glaber, in the whole universe, but in particular in France, an in Italy, "the world was covered with a white robe of churches." Thes were generally decorated with paintings and bas-reliefs now effaced by tim There are many left, however, in France and in Catalonia, the most comple being in Saint Savin near Poitiers. Romanesque painters were still inspire by the themes of Byzantine imagery. The figures of their frescoes reprodu the flat painting, rigid draperies and hieratic attitudes derived from th Christianized Near-East.

BYZANTINE SCHOOL.—13th century. Enthroned Madonna and Child.
Washington, D. C., National Gallery of Art.

Sparkling upon their background of gold, the Byzantine icons evoke the supernatural realities of an art entirely dominated by theological concepts.

PARISIAN SCHOOL, about 1373 (?).—Wilton Diptych, right panel.
London, National Gallery.

This work, which shows King Richard of England being presented to the Virgin by his patron saints, is, with its freshness of coloring and exquisite grace of line, one of the rare existing masterpieces of the aristocratic school of Paris.

FRANCO-FLEMISH ART, about 1390-1400.—St. Christopher.
Antwerp, Mayer van den Bergh Museum.

*the quality of the line evokes Paris, the unctuousness of the painting, joined
a certain naturalism native to the States of Burgundy, well demonstrates
the Franco-Flemish collaboration which marks the end of the century.*

JAN, POL AND HENNEQUIN OF LIMBURG, THE VERY RICH HOURS OF THE DUKE OF BERRY, between 1411 and 1416.—The Month of February. Chantilly, Musée Condé.

For the first time, the seasons leave their mark on the representation of Nature.

Gothic art was the national ar France during the Middle Ages. marks the complete renewal of Ch tian art at that period when, reno cing Eastern images and conce which heretofore had inspired it, European spirit created a pla system totally different from tha Asia and the Near East. It mig indeed, be said to represent "Euro revenge on Asia."

The term "Gothic" applied to dieval art, and in particular to architecture of the time, is, howe an historical error; so-called Got art is indeed but a development European Christian art, which f expressed itself in the Romane era. This new architectural ty which attained its greatest perfect between the reigns of Philippe Augu and Saint Louis —*i.e.* between 1 and 1270 A.D.—was prejudicial painting, as it allotted little or no wall space for decorative purpo This restriction stimulated the art of painting on glass. For nearly th centuries, a series of inimitable stained glass masterpieces were produced those lands where Gothic architecture flourished, of which the windows Angers, Bourges and the Sainte-Chapelle in Paris are among the me perfect examples.

A school of miniaturists also developed about this time in Paris, its far soon to spread abroad. These artists sought inspiration in stained gla their craftsmanship was both refined and delicate. Towards the middle the 13th century, under the influence of monumental art in Paris, th adopted a new style inspired by architecture and sculpture, but transpos into a linear technique of exquisite elegance. The artists now sought combine beauty of style with extreme attention to ornamentation, detail an costume. The Psalter composed for Saint Louis and members of t royal family of France, and the Liturgical Missal executed for the Sain Chapelle, are excellent examples of these new works. This art reache

AN, POL AND HENNEQUIN OF LIMBURG, THE VERY RICH HOURS OF
THE DUKE OF BERRY, between 1411 and 1416.—The Month of June.
Chantilly, Musée Condé.—*This admirable book, the most beautiful of the
Middle Ages, painted by Flemish artists for a French prince, is a synthesis of
all the currents in the European painting of that time: Italian, French, and
Flemish. Here, the landscape makes its appearance in Occidental art.*

supreme elegance at the beginning of the 14th century, with Jean Puce

It is sometimes difficult to distinguish between French and English of the period. Yet, although presenting many English traits, the Psalter the Municipal Library of Nuremberg and that of Queen Isabella at Mun are generally believed to have been executed in Paris. Queen Mar Psalter, at the British Museum, is almost certainly an early 14th cent English masterpiece.

Gradually, Gothic outline drawing was abandoned for a broader pictor treatment. The borders framing the decorated pages displayed an excessi ly rich ornamentation, much in vogue both in the East Anglian and Pa schools of miniature. This was especialy characteristic of the work of miniaturist Jean Pucelle. Doubtless the fundamental revolution in st which took place during this period was directly due to the Italian influer resulting from the political and dynastic relations of the time and a from the establishment of the Papal Court at Avignon (1309-1377). T explains, perhaps, that in one of Pucelle's masterpieces, the *Breviary Queen Jeanne of Navarre*, certain miniatures recall works of the Itali trecento.

At the end of the 14th century, French painting, which sprang from t miniature, showed signs of exhaustion. It was revitalized by the cont bution of painters from the North who, even before the Flemish sch proper had been formed, influenced the destiny of painting to such extent that one may speak of Franco-Flemish art. At the same time, t Italian influence (of which the fresco decorations of the Papal Palace Avignon were an active proving ground), extended further and furth north. All these characteristics permeate that masterpiece of miniatu art, the *Très Riches Heures du Duc de Berry* preserved at Chantil This book was painted between 1411 and 1416 by the three Limburg br thers for the Duke of Berry, uncle of Charles VI, a great patron of the ar The northern feeling for landscape is expressed here for the first time.

We know, from the texts, that the castles had halls adorned with gre fresco decorations, evocative of legends, of hunting and fishing scenes, woodland and animal life. The only example still in existence is to found in the Wardrobe Room of the Papal Palace, at Avignon. Fren art was likewise the first to nurture the art of portrait-painting: the portra of John The Good, at the Louvre, is all that remains of it today.

GIOTTO.—The Death of St. Francis of Assisi. Florence, Bardi Chapel.
Santa Croce.

*The orchestration of the gestures concentrates the dramatic interest, while the
arrangement of the masses creates an admirable and monumental equilibrium.*

ART IN ITALY
IN THE 13th AND 14th CENTURIES

THE Gothic tradition survived until the beginning of the 15th century,
when it was gradually replaced by "naturalism," especially in the
works of the Italian painters of the epoch who, seeking inspiration in
sculpture, learnt to construct living forms.

As early as the 13th century, Italy traced the way that was to be followed
by the painters of the Renaissance.

Among the immediate precursors of Giotto, the painters of Lucca and
Pisa — the Berlinghieri of Lucca and Giunta of Pisa — in the 13th century
painted works still in the Byzantine tradition, which however possess a
certain dramatic intensity of expression.

GUIDO DA SIENA.—Madonna and Child (1221?). Siena, Royal Galler

*Although still entirely Byzantine in style, this painting, whose date may
read either as 1221 or 1271, already shows the Sienese tendencies towa
tenderness and elegance.*

In Rome, Pietro Cavallini, coming to contact with the ancient assocations of the city, at once divested himself of Byzantinism the grand mosaic compositions Santa Maria di Trastevere and the frescoes of Santa Cecilia di Trastevere.

At the end of the 13th century, Cimabue, a Florentine artist who has been proclaimed by his enthusiastic fellow-citizens the Father Italian painting, proved far less free from the Byzantine tradition than Cavallini. Certain of his works timidly proclaim a new style forerunner of the great art of the 14th century.

Among the works that still exist and are generally attributed to Cimabue are a *Madonna and Child with Angels* in the National Gallery, London, and a *Madonna and Child with* twenty-six medallions set in the frame, originally in San Fransco at Pisa, now in the Louvre.

According to tradition, Cimabue was the master of Giotto, whom he discovered when Giotto was a

boy of ten, drawing the figure of a sheep with a piece of coal on a slate, while watching his father's flocks.

From the end of the 13th century to the Renaissance, Italian art is dominated by the figure of Giotto, who discovered and applied the great secret of European art : that of creating life. His frescoes in the semi-destroyed Chapel of the Arena in Padua depict the already familiar story of Christ and the Virgin. But, for the first time, these holy personages appear really alive, instead of being mere flattened figures. They possess volume; the artist has succeeded in detaching them from their background and defining them in space. Giotto could have justly claimed to be the first modern painter; he inaugurated naturalistic painting by creating independent and mobile men and women. Another outstanding innovation was to present figures in profile. Giotto's silhouettes thus acquire a personality

GIOTTO.—Christ Appearing to St. Magdalen. Fresco. Padua, Chur
of the Arena.

*The plastic vigor, which recalls the art of the sculptor, and the expressive sobrie
of the composition heighten the dramatic intensity.*

utterly lacking in the old Byzantine compositions. In the Arena frescoe
Christ is nearly always shown side-face. Indeed Giotto's figures lose son
of their power of expression when seen full-face.

Giotto shows all the characteristics of the great Italian art of the fresc
His draughtsmanship is powerful and restrained, his volumes are simplifie
his coloring is reduced to a few tones. This somewhat crude concentratio
of means enhances the intense dramatic power of his compositions. Giott
was also the creator of a decorative style in which the general rhythm of th
subjects harmonizes subtly with the architectural scheme. This is esp
cially apparent in the Church of Santa Croce in Florence, where he has repr

DDEO GADDI.—The Meeting of St. Joachim and St. Anne. Fresco, rence, Santa Croce.—*A comparison with the fresco of Giotto on page shows how his Florentine students, under the impression that they were intaining his style, really overburdened it and destroyed its dramatic quality by yielding to a taste for the picturesque.*

ted the lives of John the Baptist, Saint John the Evangelist and Saint ancis, the last fresco being no doubt painted after 1317. His decorative stem was destined to be fully developed during the Italian Renaissance l was to influence deeply the modern way of seeing.

The art of painting, as created anew by Giotto, was carried on in Italy his pupils and successors for nearly a hundred years. Many iottesques" have left on the walls of Umbria and Tuscany decorations

Duccio di Buoninsegna.—The Agony in the Garden.   Siena, Opera (
Duomo.

The large group of figures of the Passion to be found on the reverse side of
panel depicting the Enthroned Virgin, executed from 1308 to 1311,
inspired by Byzantine originals; the flexibility of the line indicates the penetr
tion of Gothic influence.   The dramatic effect here is obtained not by t
concentration of attention, as with Giotto, but by the accumulation of gestur
and expressions.

which prove the influence that the master exerted on such painters as Tadd
Gaddi, Spinello Aretino and even on Orcagna of Florence, who was al
a sculptor, and whose masterpiece, the *Golden Tabernacle of San Miche*
(1349), shows how deeply he had been impressed by Giotto's works.

The art of Siena took longer to free itself from Byzantinism, but, in t
second half of the 13th century, Guido da Siena already displays the chara
teristic grace and suavity which distinguish Siena from austere, virile Florenc

The first great master of the school was Duccio di Buoninsegna wh
although inspired by the traditional Byzantine "Virgins," painted a *Madon*
in Glory whose tender, gentle smile differs from the melancholic expressi
of her Eastern sisters.   He also expresses the pathos of pain in scenes fro
the Passion of Christ.

SIMONE MARTINI.—The Annunciation (1333). Florence, Uffizi Gallery.
Influenced by Gothic ivories, Simone Martini invents this undulating style
mannered elegance which remains to the end the essential characteristic
of the Sienese school.

AMBROGIO LORENZETTI.—The Good Government (detail). Fresco (13.
1338). Siena, Public Palace, Hall of Peace.

In his frescoes, more than in his paintings on panels, the Sienese Ambro
Lorenzetti has attempted to assimilate the robust plastic art of Giotto.

Simone Martini (Simone Memmi), whom Petrarch placed in the sa
rank as Giotto, was however the first artist to modernize the features of t
Virgin. His beautiful *Maestà*, or *Virgin in Glory*, on the wall of the gr
hall of the Municipal Palace of Siena, is reminiscent of the Notre Da
conceived by the French Gothics.

Another Sienese, Ambrogio Lorenzetti, besides painting charmi
Madonnas, decorated other rooms of the Municipal Palace of his native ci
with frescoes celebrating the *Beneficent Effects of Good Government*. On t
opposite wall, the *Disastrous Consequences of Bad Government* are also c
to his brush. These works which show the influence of Giotto, thr
an interesting light on the intense civic spirit which then animated t
Tuscans.

Tommaso da Modena.—Fra Giovanni da Schio. Fresco (1352). Treviso, Dominican Convent.

contrast to the Sienese idealism and Florentine formalism, the realism of he Lombards in the 14th century indicates perhaps a northern influence.

CIMABUE.—Madonna with Angels (about 1260). Paris, Musée du Louvre

This monumental icon, which comes from the Church of St. Francis of Pisa,
is still entirely Byzantine in spirit, but is already less rigid in style.

THE EARLY RENAISSANCE

FRA ANGELICO. — The Annunciation (detail): The Archangel Gabriel, Corto- na Church of the Jesuits.

The Annunciation of Cor- tona, with its purity of coloring and line, is one of the most perfect works of Fra Angelico.

THE term Renaissance designates that great intellectual and artistic revival which swept all European countries in the 15th and 16th centuries, and ushered in the historical period to which our own modern civilization belongs. We are, in short, the direct descendants of the Renaissance. In the Gothic countries, that is in Northern Europe, it took on the aspect of a revolution; whereas in Italy, where it had started much earlier, it continued to develop slowly and inevitably. The principle of the Renaissance is the substitution of knowledge through reason for knowledge through faith. In art this produced an ardent curiosity about nature which succeeded the unreal representations of the Middle Ages. In Italy, this intellectual rationalism was based upon the influence of Classic antiquity. The Northern countries sought in Italy their emancipation from the Middle Ages.

At the beginning of the 15th century, signs of the early Renaissance were already very apparent in Italy. Artists were no longer preoccupied solely with religious compositions, and began to turn their attention to scenes of daily life. They also brought greater care to the study of the human form. At Verona, Pisanello endowed the Gothic arabesque with a purely Italian grace. He excelled at the accurate rendition of animals, and his portraits such as that of *Lionel d'Este* at Bergamo, and of a *Princess of the House of Este* at the Louvre—recall the style of the Northern miniaturists.

Naturalism was the dominant preoccupation of Italian artists at this period. Fra Angelico, a Dominican monk whom popular fervor caused to be beatified, was both a naturalist and a mystic. Although intensely spiritual, he did not hesitate to introduce portraits into his compositions. He was and remains one of the world's great colorists, his forms subtly adapted to the mystic sentiments expressed. He treated only religious sub- jects, and it is said that he never took paint brush in hand without having first prayed with utmost fervor. Tradition adds that he was moved to tears when he painted Crucifixions.

[33]

FRA ANGELICO.—The Holy Conversation (detail). Fresco. Florence, Monastery of St. Mark.—*In the frescoes of St. Mark, he breaks away from the style of the miniature, the Gothic influence and the Sienese tendencies which characterized his early period. With Masaccio, he renews the tradition of the grand Florentine style by his well-balanced compositions, by the statuesque conception of his figures, and by his architectural backgrounds. A man of the Renaissance, he adopts the new architectural style initiated by Michelozzo.*

MASOLINO DA PANICALE.—Salome presenting the Head of St. John
the Baptist to Herodias.   Fresco.   Castiglione d'Olona,
Baptistry of the Collegiate Church.

inted in 1423 or 1424, the frescoes of this Florentine show the tradition of
otto still closely linked to the Gothic style.   The influence of Lombardy,
ere these frescoes were painted, explains perhaps this Gothic elegance.

The most celebrated of Fra Angelico's works are the series of frescoes painted for the monastery of Saint Mark at Florence (now a museum) a those executed toward the end of his life for the Chapel of Nicholas V the Vatican, whose subjects are derived from the lives of Saint Stephen a Saint Lawrence. These works show mysticism of expression, a nol harmony of composition and a fine treatment of architectural perspecti

Masolino appears as one of the important figures of 15th century F rentine art. Less famous than his pupil Masaccio, he was none the l a forerunner of the Renaissance. Although his paintings are somewl Gothic in form, he early freed himself from the influence of t "Giottesques." The study of anatomy and perspective interested h deeply. He was the author of the *Castiglione d'Olona* which, long hidc under a thick coat of paint, restored him to the place he deserves in Itali art.

With Masaccio, whom some consider the predecessor of Raphael, t first elements of modern art are clearly visible. He too was deeply prec cupied by the study of the human body; and, in order to express its power, minimized landscape. Although Masaccio died at the age of 27, he w able, far better than Masolino, to realize the harmony "of the ideal and t real, of poetry and exactitude, of grandeur and truth." He restored grand simplicity of Giotto, reacting against the growing complication Italian painting of the epoch. Masaccio's works, such as the *Polyptych the Carmine* at Pisa (1426) and the frescoes decorating the Brancacci Cha of Santa Maria del Carmine at Florence, greatly influenced success generations of painters. Among these were eminent artists such as Filip Lippi, author of the frescoes representing the life of Saint Stephen at t Cathedral of Prato; Piero della Francesca, celebrated for his Arezzo fresco Baldovinetti, "the ingenious and wise;" Benozzo Gozzoli and, final Raphael himself.

About 1440, certain painters, drawing their inspiration from sculptu sought to endow their figures with the solidity of relief and organized th composition according to the strictest rules of linear perspective. Pac di Dono, surnamed Uccello on account of his love of birds, discover and mastered the science of perspective which became his great preoccup tion. He has left three battle scenes in which he makes use of the differe attitudes of horses purely as a study in geometrical masses.

Andrea del Castagno carried still further the illusionism of relief, even giving his figures the appearance of bronze statues, as in the *Last Supper* Santa Apollonia. In the Piero della Francesca frescoes of the *Legend of Cross* at Arezzo, the personages in their strange, sculptural isolation, se as withdrawn as sleep-walkers.

The influence of sculpture produced extremes of style in the paintings

GENTILE DA FABIRANO.—Adoration of the Magi. Florence, Uffizi Gallery

The famous Adoration of the Magi, of the Uffizi Gallery, painted in 1423 for the Church of the Holy Trinity at Florence, is one of the most poetic expressions of the picturesque and princely style which resulted from the international art of 1400, and which reigned in Northern and Central Italy, while, in Florence, the plastic revolution of the Renaissance was developing.

PISANELLO.—St. Anthony and St. George. London, National Gallery

The old dreams of medieval wonders find expression in the aristocratic wo[rld] of Pisanello; the pure elegance of his drawing is the heritage of Goth[ic] civilization.

Fʀᴀ Fɪʟɪᴘᴘᴏ Lɪᴘᴘɪ.—Madonna and Child. Washington, D. C., National
Gallery of Art.

student of Fra Angelico, Fra Filippo Lippi, defrocked Carmelite monk,
secularizes" religious painting. The face of the Madonna is that of his
istress, Lucrezia Buti, a nun with whom he had run away. The infant
esus resembles their son, Filippino Lippi, who also became a painter
and monk.

MASACCIO—St. Peter and the Tribute to Cesar. Fresco. Florence, Carmine

In the frescoes of the Carmine of Florence, Masaccio leads the Florentine scho
back to its real tradition, that of Giotto, whose dramatic power and monument
expression he recaptures, but with a certain increased contraction and tensi
which correspond to the fever of research in the 15th century.

the School of Ferrara by Francesco Cossa, Cosimo Tura and others who
overwrought art can be compared to that of the Germanic painters.

At the end of the 15th century, the Florentine School, which had been t
initiator of the Renaissance, saw the blossoming of numerous talents.　T
tradition of the sculptural style ended with Verrocchio, a painter, goldsmi
and sculptor who was to become the master of Leonardo da Vinci.　T
Pollaiuolo brothers endowed their painting with the somewhat dry mann
of the goldsmith's art, which they also practised.　The incisive line
Florence produced its finest arabesques with the advent of Sandro Botticel
a high-strung, dramatic artist who painted melancholic Madonnas, b
who was one of the first to adopt profane subjects from mythology.　
him we owe the *Birth of Venus*, the *Primavera* (or *Allegory of Sprin*
and his *Allegory of Calumny*, the latter an effort to reconstitute aft

ᴀɴᴅʀᴇᴀ ᴅᴇʟ Cᴀsᴛᴀɢɴᴏ.—Portrait of a Florentine. Washington, D. C.,
Andrew Mellon Collection. National Gallery of Art.

*e sharp, clear-cut style of Andrea del Castagno, inspired by the influence
'he workers in bronze and gold, well suits the proud and haughty expression
of his figures.*

GIOVANNI DI PAOLO.—The Presentation in the Temple. New York,
Metropolitan Museum.

In the work of Giovanni di Paolo, the Sienese style, with its brilliant colori
and undulating line, takes on a mannered and nervous aspect which expres
the decadence of the school.

PAOLO UCCELLO.—The Rout of San Romano. London, National Gallery.

Everything in this work serves as pretext for an analysis of form in space: studies of foreshortening, problems of perspective, etc. The forms of the horses and men in armor are reduced, in accordance with the artist's sense of abstraction, to the generating lines of geometry.

descriptions of ancient authors a painting of the Greek Apelles. With the advent of Ghirlandaio and Benozzo Gozzoli, extreme intellectual naturalism gave way to picturesqueness and anecdote. The frescoes painted by Ghirlandaio for Santa Maria Novella in Florence, depicting the lives of the Virgin and of Saint John the Baptist, are faithful renditions of Florentine life in the 15th century—the actual settings, costumes, architecture and decorative details familiar to the contemporaries of Lorenzo di Medici and Savonarola. Gozzoli gave free rein to a vivid imagination in his paintings describing the *Life of Noah* at the Campo Santo of Pisa.

The end of the 15th century, as the period when all the Italian schools were formed, saw the flowering of a splendid artistic activity. In Tuscany, Filippo Lippi was putting the last touches to the famous Brancacci Chapel, Cosimo Rosselli was working at his *Crossing of the Red Sea* in the Sistine Chapel, while Sandro Botticelli was proving himself as one of the most gifted creators of the Renaissance.

The Umbrian School graduated from mere craftsmanship with Pietro Vannucci, better known as Perugino. He devoted himself exclusively to

PIERO DELLA FRANCESCA.—The Nativity.   London, National Gallery

Highly influenced by the monumental plastic art of the Florentines, the Umbr
is inspired to expressions of power and pride; he gives to his figures a cert
monolithic form.

religious subjects in which sentiment dominated science.   During his lifeti
he enjoyed great popularity.   He is said to have frequented the studio
Verrocchio, where he learned to soften the contours of his rather arch
drawing by the skilful use of fine shading.   His coloring was golden a
the attitudes of his figures full of grace.   Unfortunately, Perugino was
productive; he lacked variety and perhaps inspiration, and was content
repeat himself endlessly.

Likewise an Umbrian, Luca Signorelli makes a complete contrast
Perugino.   A forerunner of Michelangelo, he was preoccupied with muscu
beauty and athletic prowess.   The dramatic power of his composition v

DOMENICO VENEZIANO.—Portrait of a Young Woman.
Berlin, Kaiser Friedrich Museum.

e influence of the medallist's art on these portraits of the Quattrocento is
ceptible in the enchased contours which one finds inscribed on the background.

ALESSIO BALDOVINETTI.—Madonna :
Child. Paris, Musée du Louvre.

A work of precise and accomplished bea
which surpasses the analytical perio
the generation of Castagno and Ucce

only surpassed by Michelangelo, ν
studied carefully Signorelli's frescoe:
the cathedral of Orvieto represent
the Last Judgment.

The School of Venice was slow
freeing itself from the Byzantine
fluence which dominated it entirely
the 14th century. As early as 136₅
Paduan named Guarienti had pain·
a *Paradise* for the Ducal Palace. Ant·
Vivarini, who trained many pupils
whose large and harmonious comp·
tions were placed in fine architectι
settings, combined the manner of !
zantium with the influence of the sculptural style of Florence.   The Venet
School owed a great deal to a Sicilian painter called Antonello da Messi·
who may have visited Flanders and had in any case acquainted hims
with the technique of Van Eyck's painting in oils.   Having settled
Venice in 1475, he introduced there this technique which was to change
destiny of the Venetian school.

However, it was the Bellinis who freed Venetian painting from its arch·
manner.   The head of the family, Jacopo Bellini, still a Byzantinist, trave·
to Florence and to Padua to familiarize himself both with naturali
and antiquity.   Eventually he liberated Venetian art from the influence
the East.   His sons, Gentile and Giovanni, opened up the two diverg·
paths which Venetian art was to follow.   Giovanni was attached to ·
expression of ideal beauty in his Madonnas; he was appreciative of nat·
and was to be the creator of Venetian landscape.   His brother Gentile ·
attracted by picturesque effects and his religious paintings are pretexts
the rendering of crowds and processions on the Piazza of Venice.   ·
brothers' authority asserted itself after they had learnt the technique of
painting from Antonello da Messina, which in turn they passed on to th·
numerous pupils.   Giovanni Bellini, who lived until 1516, was the master
Giorgione and Titian.   From his studio emerged the art of Venice in ·
15th century.

In the North of Italy, other centers of artistic culture had appeared, su·

ERCOLE DE ROBERTI.—Ginevra Bentivoglio.   Washington, D. C.,
National Gallery of Art.

mented and dramatic, the style of the school of Ferrara indicates perhaps
Germanic influence, which diminishes with Ercole de Roberti, the last
great master of the school.

ANDREA DEL VERROCCHIO.—The Baptism of Christ.   Florence,
Uffizi Gallery.

Both goldsmith and worker in bronze, Andrea Verrocchio transposes in
rare paintings the plastic qualities of the art which he practiced most readi
The bodies of Christ and St. John reveal a keen analysis of anatomy wh
contrasts with the gentleness of the two angels and with the hazy landsca
background for which his student Leonardo da Vinci is responsible.

SANDRO BOTTICELLI.—Giovanni Degli Albizzi and the Three Graces (detail). Fresco. Paris, Musée du Louvre.

the work of Botticelli, the last great master of Florence, the extreme tenseness line, the melancholy expressions and the affected attitudes express the nervous agitation of the declining school.

[49]

BENOZZO GOZZOLI.—The Procession of the Magi (detail). Fresco. Florence, Ricardi Palace. — *Abandoning the plastic research of the preced generation, Benozzo Gozzoli seems to return to the past finding his inspira in the picturesque and narrative style of Gentile da Fabriano whose Adora of the Magi fascinated him.*

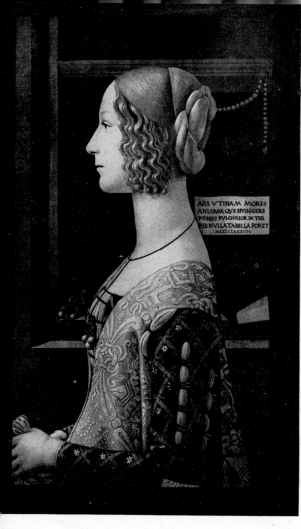

GHIRLANDA-
IO. — Portrait
of Giovanna
Albizzi Torna-
buoni. Edsel
Ford Coll.

*A comparison
with the figures
on pages 45
and 47, also
seen in profile,
shows how
much the bour-
geois tone of
Ghirlandaio's
art causes it to
lose in quality
of style, even
if it does gain
in realism.*

ARS VTINAM MORES
ANIMVM QVE EFFINGERE
POSSES PVLCHRIOR IN TER
RIS NVLLA TABELLA FORET
MCCCLXXXVIII

t Padua, closely linked with Venice, where Andrea Mantegna, once a
oherd like Giotto, became one of the greatest painters of all time.
ntegna was a pupil of Francesco Squarcione, founder of the School of
ua, a great archæologist, who had visited Greece, Italy and the East. He
municated to Mantegna his passion for classical antiquity. Heir to the

VITTORE CARPACCIO.—Portrait of a Young Knight.   Lugano,
Schloss Rohoncz Collection.—*In Venice, Vittore Carpaccio prolongs u*
the beginning of the 16th century the fabulous and legendary spirit of
Middle Ages, but his power of observation delights in the varied specta
which the cosmopolitan city of the lagoon offers.

ANDREA MANTEGNA.—The Martyrdom of St. James. Padua, Eremitani.

It was at Padua, rather than at Florence, that the most beautiful synthesis of the plastic research of the Quattrocento was realized, by Mantegna. He conceived his paintings as a sculptor, and yet, coming from the North, he was easily fascinated by the many aspects of Nature.

GIOVANNI BELLINI.—The Transfiguration. Naples, National Museu...
This painting is one of the most majestic expressions of that classic sere...
   which 15th century Venetian art attained thanks to Giovanni Bellini.

sculptural style of the Florentine painters, Mantegna added to it his sens...
color.   Learned in anatomy, his figures all have a lofty and proud bear...
The cartoons of his celebrated *Triumph of Cæsar*, which were bought...
Charles I in 1627 and later transferred to Hampton Court, are in the s...
of bas-reliefs.   His finest works, the *Life of Saint James* in the Chapel of...
Eremitani at Padua, was unfortunately destroyed during the last ...
Mantegna's influence was widespread, reaching as far as Southern Italy...
even Germany, where Dürer and Holbein felt its effects.   He was a mast...
the art of foreshortening and aimed at a picturesque naturalism based...
science, perspective and anatomy.

SANDRO BOTTICELLI.—The Birth of Venus. Florence, Uffizi Gallery.

Botticelli is one of the first artists who resolutely treated pagan subjects; at the end of his life he abandoned them under the influence of the reformer monk, Savonarola.

THE MASTER OF FLEMALLE.
—Portrait of a Man. Berlin,
State Museum.

THE artistic brilliance of Flanders in
first half of the 15th century rivaled t
of Italy. In the 15th century, the Sch
of Burgundy or Bruges could compete s
cessfully with the most celebrated Ital
schools. The Duke of Burgundy, Phili
le Bon, was the patron of Jan van Eyck,
founder of the celebrated Flemish Schoo
painting.

The Van Eyck brothers, Hubert a
Jan, revolutionized the technique of art
the discovery of oil painting; or, to be m
exact, it should be said that they succee
in mingling oil with colors more happ
than had been done until then. They l
also, after long and patient research
discovered a siccative varnish which, wh
spread over the paintings, greatly accelerated their drying. They a
knew how to lay on colors in thin and transparent coats one on top
the other, thus producing a wider range of tones and gradations.
one was better qualified than Jan van Eyck to take advantage of
infinite resources of his discovery. Long before the Venetians, he was
creator of landscape and of aerial perspective—that is, of the means wh
suggests depth by graduating tones according to distance. He convey
hallucinating impression of reality. Every detail of his compositions
rendered with a precision that has never been surpassed.

His first master was his elder brother Hubert, who died while work
with Jan on the *Triptych of the Adoration of the Lamb*, in the church
Saint Bavon at Ghent. Alone, Jan van Eyck finished the work, one of
world's masterpieces. The realistic tendencies of the school are visi
in the types represented. The picture was exhibited publicly in Ghen
May 1432, and exerted great influence.

Jan van Eyck was a great portraitist, as one can see by the persona
who figure in his works whose dominant characteristics he renders vig
ously. As a religious painter, he shows no less concern for realism;

N Van Eyck.—Jan Arnolfini and Jeanne de Chenany his wife. 1434.
London, National Gallery.

JAN VAN EYCK.—Portrait of Margaret Van Eyck, wife of the painter 14.
(detail). Bruges, Communal Museum.

*Thanks to his extraordinary power of observation, aided by a skilful techniq
Jan Van Eyck succeeded in representing the life-like qualities of the face w
an intensity that has never been attained after him.*

irgins are young Flemish girls, whom he scarcely idealizes. The persons
rounding them are copied from nature; the background often consists of
idscapes painted with great accuracy.

It is impossible to mention all the artists who followed in the wake of
n Eyck and adopted the new Flemish technique. Painting flourished
Flanders, where it became almost a national industry during the 15th
itury. The immediate successor of Van Eyck was Rogier van der Weyden
Roger de la Pasture, who became the leader of the Flemish School.
.s works, austerely presented, are remarkable for their force of expression.
: settled in Brussels five years before Philippe le Bon, having annexed
.abant, and made that city one of his favorite residences. Van der Weyden
erted considerable influence both in Germany and in his own country.

The power of the House of Burgundy continued to grow and Flemish
inting reached its highest point at the climax of that power. In 1473,
.arles the Bold, last Duke of Burgundy, aspired to be proclaimed King by
nperor Frederic II. At the same time, Justus of Ghent was called to
bino by Duke Federigo of Montefeltre and Van der Goes painted his
nous triptych of the *Adoration of the Shepherds* for the Portinari family
Florence.

One of Van der Weyden's most illustrious disciples was Hans Memlinc*,
Rhenish origin, who, after having studied at Cologne, doubtless frequent-
de la Pasture's studio. He may even have collaborated with the great
emish painter. His best known works are at Bruges, where he spent the
:ater part of his life. Memlinc, who painted for monks and nuns,
pressed from the heart his religious faith; his Madonnas and saints are full
sweetness, but his works no longer possess the tragic grandeur and mystic
tiness of Rogier.

The Low Countries, which were later to become one of the greatest
:istic centers of the world, were in the 15th century singularly devoid of
:-eminent artists. Most of them, such as Dirk Bouts of Haarlem, worked
Flanders. One, however, ranks as the most curious original of all time.
: was Jerome van Aeken, or Hieronymus Bosch as he is generally called,
10 lived in the second half of the century and worked at Bois-le-Duc. As a
:irist, he was greatly in advance of his time, though his fantastic visions
d terrifying concepts were characteristic of the Middle Ages. His
rks were much admired in Spain, especially by the morbid Philip II, and
/eral of his greatest pictures such as the *Hay Cart* can be seen in Madrid.

* Memlinc, also Memling.

HUBERT AND JAN VAN EYCK.—Altar-piece of the Adoration of the Lamb. Central panel: The Adoration of the Lamb. Ghent, Church of St. Bavon.

For the first time Paradise is not depicted as an imaginary realm but rather in a realistic manner as a

PETRUS CHRISTUS.—The Legend of St. Eligius. 1449.
New York, Philip Lehman Collection.

ss *forcefully, Petrus Christus, an imitator of Jan Van Eyck, attempts to*
ress the atmosphere of an interior; like Van Eyck, he uses a convex mirror
(see page 57) *in order to suggest what cannot be seen directly.*

ROGIER VAN DER WEYDEN.—Madonna and Child.   Private Collection

The art of Rogier van der Weyden is deeply Christian; the suffering Vir
and Child are the two figures which appear most frequently in his painti
These Madonnas formed a diptych with the portrait of the donor, which
plains their position.   The angular drawing is akin to the Middle Ages.

IER VAN DER WEYDEN.—Portrait of a Lady.   John D. Rockefeller Jr. Coll.

*portraits of Weyden do not have the life-like intensity of those of Van
; austere and melancholy, they are more spiritual and remain profoundly
Christian.*

Rogier van der Weyden.—Christ with the Virgin and St. John
Evangelist. Paris, Musée du Louvre.

This painting is the central panel of a small triptych, for use in the h
commissioned by the Braque family whose arms are found on the ou
panels. It is a masterpiece of the artist's maturity (about 1450); alth
using realistic means, he succeeds in creating a spiritual expression as
as that of Byzantine art. The harsh style of his early period is here some
softened, perhaps as a result of a trip to Italy which Rogier made from 1
to 1451.

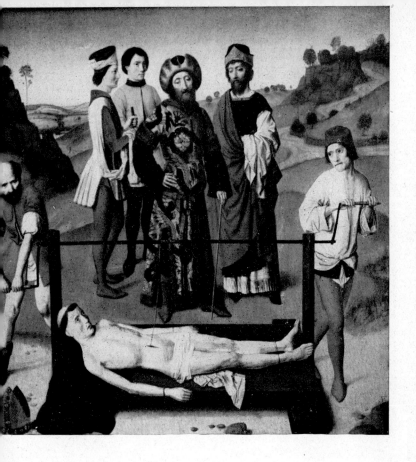

DIRK BOUTS.—The Martyrdom of St. Erasmus (1449).   Louvain,
Church of St. Peter.

*ifferent to the moral character of the subjects he depicts, Bouts paints this
htful martyrdom with surprising passiveness.   Only plastic problems
rest him : the position of forms in space, the perspective of the landscape, etc.*

MEMLINC.—Diptych of Martin van Nieuwenhoven (1487). Left pane
The Madonna (detail). Bruges, Hospital of St. John.

*Memlinc's conception of the Madonna is derived from that of Weyden;
Memlinc softens and idealizes his Madonna so as to endow her with gre
beauty. Note the mirror which enlarges the size of the room.*

RK BOUTS.—Altar-piece of the Lord's Supper (1464-1468). Central section:
The Last Supper. Louvain, St. Peter's Church.

is painting is composed with the same rigor common to the Italian masters.
in the Last Supper by Leonardo da Vinci, everything converges toward the
d of Christ, whose elongated nose is situated on the central axis of the picture.

ALBRECHT BOUTS.—Christ Crowned with Thorns.   Museum of Düsseldo

*At Louvain, the son of Bouts, Albrecht, continued the tradition of pious ima
ry: figures of the Madonna and of Christ crowned with thorns, most often
the form of diptychs.*

Bruges Master of the Legend of St. Ursula.—The Legend of St. Ursula
(detail).   Bruges, Convent of the Black Sisters.

*The Master of the Legend of St. Ursula is original in his popular spirit which
is quite rare at a time when painting in Bruges, under the influence of
Memlinc, was tending to become more aristocratic and refined.*

MEMLINC.—The Beheading of St. John the Baptist.   Panel of the Mys
Marriage.   Bruges, Hospital of St. John.

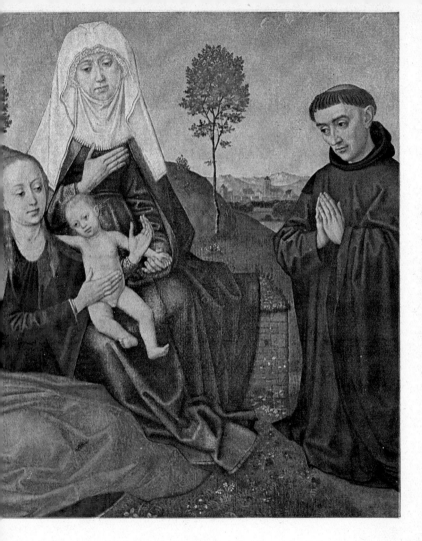

GO VAN DER GOES.—The Virgin and St. Anne (detail).   Brussels, Royal
seums. *At the end of the century, Hugo van der Goes of Ghent, thanks to his*
ular enthusiasm and ardent temperament, gave a new vigor to Flemish art
ch was becoming dull and uninteresting in the hands of the students of
Rogier van der Weyden.

HUGO VAN DER GOES.—The Temptation of Adam and Eve.   Vienna
Kunst historisches Museum.

The study of the nude goes back to the Altar-piece of the Lamb, by Van Eyck, wh
contains two large figures of Adam and Eve.   Here, the artist's realism ma
it awkward for him to depict an imaginary figure such as the beguiling serp

JEROME BOSCH.—The Temptation of St. Anthony.   Private Collection.

With his extraordinary imagination, Jerome Bosch has depicted a troubled world of nightmares and the powers of Evil by means of strange and unusual monsters which seem to be devil-like caricatures of the Creation.

JEROME BOSCH.—The Ship of Fools (detail). Paris, Musée du Louvre.

The Ship of Fools is a symbol of the dissoluteness of the five senses; this painti
was inspired by a satirical work on the society of the time, published in 14
by Josse Bade.

JEROME BOSCH.—The Hay Cart. Central Panel. Madrid, Escorial.

e hay is the symbol of worldly goods over whose possession the frantic figures
seen quarreling and killing. The cart rolls irresistibly toward the
ss, while under the very wheels, which are to crush them, the depraved monks
laymen continue to struggle. In the center foreground, a puller of teeth,
pockets filled with hay, works on a screaming patient. One notes the figure
liar who is spreading false doctrines. On the left, a magician and gypsies
their seductive trade. Each of Bosch's pictures is a vast symbolic ency-
edia in which are assembled ancient beliefs in hidden mysteries, in astrology
and magic.

GERMANIC ART
IN THE 14th AND 15th CENTURIES

N the Middle Ages, Germanic Europe was an artistic center. The princess who, on the death of her husband Otho II in 983, settled in Cologne,
l drawn to her court not only German but also many Byzantine painters.
n the 14th century, Cologne became an important center of religious
nting (Altar of the Clarissas) having benefited by the intercrossed
uences of Viennese painting and French miniature art. Rhenish mys-
sm extended in the 15th century to the valley of the Middle Rhine and

SCHOOL OF CENTRAL GERMANY.—Joseph Recognizing Mary as the Mother
of God (about 1350). Berlin, Deutsches Museum.

Master Bertram.—Altar of St. Peter's (detail: Rest During the Flight into Egypt.) Hamburg, Kunsthalle.

*r the end of the 14th century, there appeared in the Hanse region that
iliar and popular spirit which is one of the charms of medieval German art.*

MASTER FRANCKE.—The Betrayal of St. Barbara (about 1420).
Helsingfors, National Museum.

*The art of Master Francke, who painted at Hamburg, is inspired by
Franco-Flemish miniatures of 1400, but shows a dramatic intensity an
popular realism which reveals one aspect of the German temperame*

STER OF THE MIDDLE RHINE. (about 1420).—The Garden of Paradise
(detail). Frankfurt, Staedel Institute.

is tiny painting, precious as an enamel, shows the Virgin resting in a
sed garden in the midst of several saints who are amusing the Infant Jesus.
eflects the naïve dreams of the Rhenish monks, and especially of the nuns.

CONRAD VON SOEST (Westphalia, about 1420).—The Death of Mary
(detail).   Dortmund, St. Mary's Church.

*Prompted by their sense of the supernatural, the mystic painters of the Rhinel
took pleasure in portraying angels, whom they depict as unreal, quiver
creatures somewhat like birds.   Here the Gothic arabesque finds its hig
expression of irrealism.*

STEPHAN LOCHNER.—The Altar of the Three Kings. Central panel:
The Adoration of the Magi (detail). Cologne Cathedral.

*e "Dombild" of the Cathedral of Cologne accompanies the sumptuous
ine of the Three Magi whose relics Cologne was believed to possess. It
hrough a reference in a story-book by Albrecht Dürer that the painter of
this retable is known.*

MASTER OF ST. VERONICA.—The Veil of St. Veronica. Munich,
Pinakothek

The Master of Veronica is half-way between the linear manner of the
century and the agreeable and delicately shaded painting of Lochner.

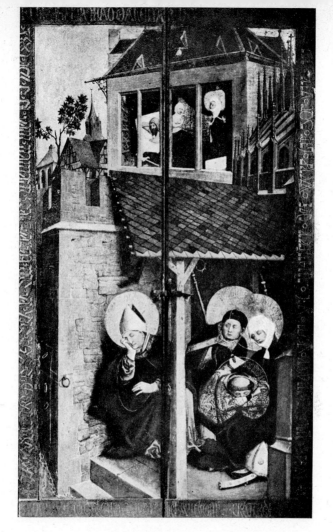

AS MOSER (Constance).—The Sleep of the Saints of Provence (detail of the Altar-piece of the Parish Church of Tiefenbronn, 1431).

Southern Germany, under the Burgundian influence from Dijon, there
loped a realistic style which, contrary to the Rhenish traditions, sought
to obtain a density of volume and the expression of space.

CONRAD WITZ. (Constance and Basel).—David and Abigail (detail of the A
piece of the Mirror of the Salvation, about 1435). Basel, National Muse

The stocky figures of Conrad Witz, inspired by the art of Dijon, cast sha
on the uniform background, like statues of bronze, which they resemble als
their firmness.

SCHOOL OF NUREMBERG (about 1440).—Altar of the Tucher family.
Nuremberg, St. Mary's Church.

Westphalia. At the beginning of this century Conrad von Soest was
finest representative. The painting of the Hanseatic cities (Master
ncke at Hamburg) is of a rougher primitivism. The mystical strain
d out and became more earthy at Cologne, with Stephan Lochner, who
nted his famous triptych, the *Adoration of the Magi*, between 1430 and
o. Lochner's coloring is delicate, his Madonnas frail and mysterious.
already these paintings betray the growing influence of Flemish realism
ch put emphasis on the rendition of accessories.
Whereas in the 14th century the influence of Italy ascended the valley
the Rhine, in the 15th it was Flemish influence which flowed down the
r; it thus penetrated into Germany from the South, thanks to the
espread diffusion of culture from Dijon. This influence ushered in the
tere, Gothic style of Rogier van der Weyden, which was to be elaborated
the Germans. It is manifested at Cologne in the works of several painters

CONRAD WITZ.—The Miraculous Draught of Fishes (1444). Geneva,
Museum of the History of Art.

Instead of placing the scene in imaginary surroundings, the realist Con
Witz uses the setting of Lake Geneva; on the right can be seen Mount Sal
then the Mole and the ridge of the Voirons, and in the background Mont-Bla

who have remained anonymous (The Master of the Death of Mary,
Master of Saint Severinus). In Alsace, in Bavaria and in Southern Germa
the style of Van der Weyden encountered another Flemish current, ag
from Dijon, bringing with it certain attributes of its school of sculptu
which had been created by Claas Sluter. In turn, in Switzerland,
Dijon current produced Conrad Witz, whose stocky figures seem hewr
bronze. It is apparent in Swabia and Bavaria, in the works of paint
such as Lucas Moser or Hans Multscher. The latter contrasts reali

STEPHAN LOCHNER.—Altar of the Three Kings. Exterior wing:
The Annunciation (detail: The Virgin). Cologne Cathedral.

*native of Swabia, Stephan Lochner accomplishes a paradoxical synthesis
between the plastic spirit of Southern German art and the Gothic idealism of
the Rhine.*

HANS MULTSCHER (Ulm).—Christ Lifting the Cross (detail).
Upper-Swabia, Wolfegg Castle.

The plastic instinct of Multscher, who was also a sculptor, is expressed in th
work; the round faces are borrowed from the popular Swabian type.

(which is one of the aspects of Germanic pessimism) with the suavity
the Rhenish schools. In the Tyrol, the influence of Mantegna converge
with the Dijon current in the works of Michael Pacher.

The two Flemish currents, that of Rogier van der Weyden and that
Dijon, join in Franconia to create the Nuremberg School. The most signi:
cant of its primitive works is the Tucher altar-piece, executed towards 14;
for the Church of Our Lady of Nuremberg. This comprises three scenes: a
Annunciation, a *Crucifixion* and a *Resurrection*. Hans Pleydenwurff, wl
died in 1472, attained a great reputation which extended even as far
Galicia, where many of his works are to be found. His best known pain
ings are *The Crucifixions* of Munich and Nuremberg.

MASTER OF THE LIFE OF MARY (Cologne, about 1460).—The Birth of
the Virgin. Munich, Pinakothek.

*tender spirit and feminine sensibility of Cologne are continued, after
...ner's death, in the works of Romanesque style, executed under the influence
of Weyden and Bouts.*

...ichael Wolgemut was the last of the primitive painters of the Nurem-
... School. A pupil of Pleydenwurff, he inherited his studio, which turned
... a great number of paintings. Among his pupils was Albrecht Dürer who
... Wolgemut's death, headed the Nuremberg School in the 16th century.
...t Colmar, Martin Schongauer (1440-1488) was probably the pupil of
...pard Isenmann. Schongauer was influenced by the works of Van der
...den, whom he imitated in the long, angular forms of his figures, and
... stiff, heavy folds of their draperies. The suave influence of the Rhine
...nates him in *The Madonna with the Rosebush* in the Church of Saint Martin
...olmar, painted in 1473.

MASTER OF THE MIDDLE RHINE. (about 1420).—The Garden of Parad (detail). Frankfurt, Staedel Institute.

The painting of Schongauer on page 91 is inspired by the same pure id theme as the Garden of Paradise, but Flemish realism is less suited than Rhenish style to that mystic expression.

MARTIN SCHONGAUER (Colmar).—The Madonna with the Rosebush
(detail).   1473.   Colmar, St. Martin.

*influence of Rogier van der Weyden is perceptible in this painting whose
sharp line reveals the temperament of the copper-engraver.*

MICHAEL PACHER (Tyrol).—The Resurrection of Lazarus (1481).
St. Wolfgang, Church of the Presbytery.

*The exaggerated vanishing perspective and the sculptural quality of the fig
here are due to the influence of Mantegna, which easily penetrated into
frontier region of the Tyrol.*

UQUET.—The Baptism of Christ.
niature. Paris, Bibliothèque
Nationale.

THE disasters and miseries caused by the Hundred Years' War hampered in France the development of an art which had shown glowing promise. Paris being occupied by the English, French artists transported themselves, their goods and chattels to Bourges, Dijon and Avignon.

It was thus during the 15th century that the school of Tours sprang into existence, the Loire valley having become the new residence of the court of France. Jean Fouquet (1415-1483) was its master *par excellence*. He worked for Charles VII and Louis XI and went to Italy where he painted the portrait of Pope Eugenius IV. An accomplished portraitist, he was much appreciated by the Italians themselves. His likenesses of *Charles VII* and of *Juvenal des Ursins* in the Louvre, and of *Etienne Chevalier* in the Berlin Museum are the best known. The famous *Virgin* of the Antwerp Museum, generally ascribed to him, is supposed to be the portrait of Agnes Sorel, the King's mistress. The miniatures that he painted to order for Books of Hours (he Book of Hours of *Étienne Chevalier*) are rendered like full-size pictures d show the feeling for landscape peculiar to the French. The influence the Renaissance is already apparent in Jean Fouquet, who freed nself both from the linear manner and the complications of the Gothic. At Aix-en-Provence, "Good King René," who himself liked to wield the int-brush, encouraged the creation of an artistic center in which the influence the North and of Italy were both represented. Nicolas Froment execu- l for the Cathedral of Saint Sauveur, at Aix, a large picture representing the rning Bush. This is flanked by panels on which the King and his wife anne de Laval, figure under the protection of different saints. Another his works, *The Resurrection of Lazarus*, is at the Uffizi in Florence, and ows clearly the influence of the Italian School.

GREAT HOURS OF ROHAN.—The Flight into Egypt. Paris,
Bibliothèque Nationale.

*Executed without doubt in Paris about 1425, this manuscript still shows
influence of the Very Rich Hours of the Duke of Berry, but with a mov
violence which denotes a very personal temperament.*

MASTER OF THE CŒUR D'AMOUR ÉPRIS.—Heart in front of the Magic
Fountain.   Vienna, State Library.

*Master, who, about 1460, illuminated this allegorical treatise written by
King René; is a kindred spirit of Fouquet; like him, he has the characteristics of the Renaissance as well as a keen feeling for landscape.*

vignon, the papal city, continued in the 15th century to be a crossroad
re painters met from every land.   Despite this, its school of painting
a very individual style, marked both by the influence of sculpture and a
e of grandeur.   Enguerrand Quarton, who recalls to a certain degree
Angelico, painted a *Triumph of the Virgin*, which is preserved in the
oital of Villeneuve-lès-Avignon.   Finer still is the *Avignon Pietà*, now at
Louvre, one of the highest expressions of the mystical spirit and one of
greatest masterpieces of painting.   Unfortunately it is anonymous.
ccording to certain testimonies of the time, one of the most important
ach artists of the late 15th century was one Jean Perréal.   He was
son of a painter of Louis XI.   Louis XII took him to Italy and

SCHOOL OF AMIENS. (1437).—The Ministry of the Virgin (detail). P
Musée du Louvre. *This picture is one of the works executed each year fo
brotherhood or "puy" of Notre Dame, after a poem submitted in competi
It indicates the prolongation of the art of the* Very Rich Hours, *withou
influence of the* Van Eycks, *although the* Altar-piece of the Lamb
already been completed when the Ministry *was painted.*

MASTER OF THE ANNUNCIATION OF AIX (1443).—The Annunciation, central panel. Aix-en-Provence, Church of the Madeleine.

missioned him to depict the principal events of the Italian campaign. is likely that Jean Perréal was the eminent and mysterious Master of lins or painter of the Bourbons, to whom have been attributed several ks which seem clearly related one to the other. The finest of these is Retable of the Cathedral of Moulins (1498), representing the *Virgin and d Surrounded by Angels,* which recalls Ghirlandaio or Memlinc.

the North of France, in Picardy, at Valenciennes (a city which was Flemish) painting remained under the rule of neighboring Flanders. le French painting in the 15th century shone with a lesser brilliance other arts (particularly tapestry), at least it maintained its rank in the European ensemble.

ENGUERRAND QUARTON.—The Coronation of the Virgin.
Villeneuve-lès-Avignon, Civil Hospice.

This picture was painted for the Chartreuse of Villeneuve-lès-Avignon u
a contract, dated 1453, with Enguerrand Quarton, a native of Laon.
style is very close to that of the Pietà of Avignon.

SCHOOL OF AVIGNON (about 1460).—Pietà. Paris, Musée du Louvre.

masterpiece of the French School of the Middle Ages, this painting has
mained anonymous despite the extensive research made in an effort to discover
author. It is related to the works of the Catalonian School, but it is un-
estionably French by its restraint in the expression of feeling. The influence
Rogier van der Weyden is also perceptible; the composition is conceived in
sculptural manner, like all the works of the School of Avignon. Like the
ronation of the Virgin by Enguerrand Quarton, this painting comes from the
artreuse of Villeneuve-lès-Avignon; a Carthusian priest is shown praying
at the left of the picture.

SCHOOL OF AVIGNON (about 1460).—Pietà. (detail: Head of the Virgin)
Paris, Musée du Louvre.

The theme of the grief of Mary, weeping over the body of her son placed up
her lap, originates in the "Meditations on the Life of Christ," composed
the end the 14th century by a Franciscan monk (the pseudo-Bonaventure
It is in France that the theme reaches its highest spiritual expression. T
Virgin is shown here resolving her grief in prayer.

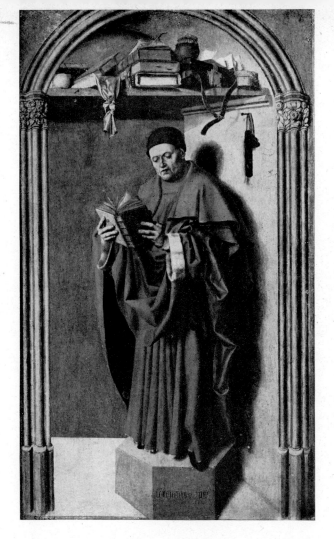

THE MASTER OF THE ANNUNCIATION OF AIX.—The Prophet Jeremiah.
Aix-en-Provence, Church of the Madeleine.

This painting is a detatched panel of The Annunciation *preserved at the
Madeleine in Aix (p. 97); it is related to the "Burgundian" art of Jan Van
Eyck and Claas Sluter.*

JEAN FOUQUET.—The Marriage of the Virgin (Book of Hours of Étienn
Chevalier). Chantilly, Condé Museum.

*Here Fouquet shows his taste for antiquity: he takes his inspiration for th
setting of the scene from the Arch of Triumph of Constantine which he ha
seen in the Forum at Rome.*

JEAN FOUQUET.—Madonna and Child. Antwerp, Royal Museum
of Fine Arts.

s picture was part of a diptych whose other panel, at Berlin, shows Étienne
alier in prayer. For the Virgin, Fouquet painted the face of the King's
mistress, Agnès Sorel.

SIMON MARMION.—Altar-piece of St. Bertin (detail, about 1459). Be
Kaiser Friedrich Museum.

SCHOOL OF BURGUNDY.—Portrait of a Man. Haarlem, Kœnigs Collection.
*This picture reveals the influence of the portraits of Rogier van der Weyden,
whose subjects are shown praying before the Virgin.*

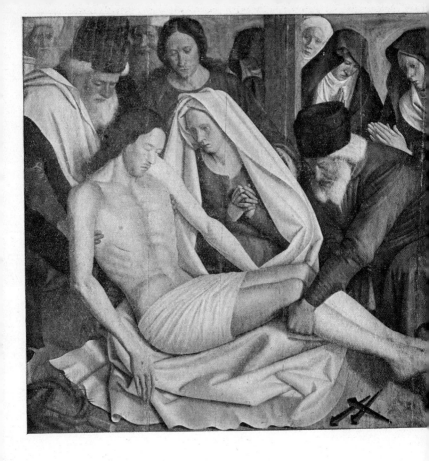

SCHOOL OF FOUQUET.—Pietà. Touraine. Parish Church of Nouans.

*Compared with the Pietà of Avignon, this Descent from the Cross shows
the difference which separates the school of the Loire from that of Avigno
The painters of the Loire seek primarily a monumental composition, tho
of Provence a dramatic intensity.*

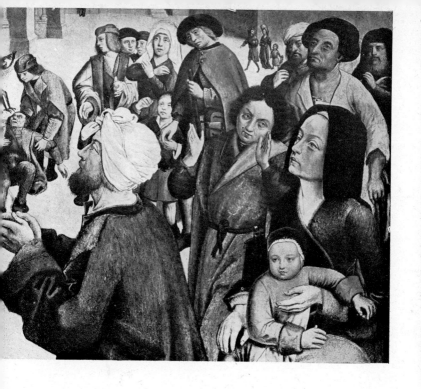

MASTER OF ST. GILES.—St. Rémi Blessing the People in the Square f Notre-Dame (detail). New York, George Wildenstein Collection.

*believed that the Master of St. Giles, who painted at the end of the century,
have been a Flemish artist living in Paris. The influence of Hugo van
oes is perceptible in his pictures. He undoubtedly worked in Paris, for, in
intings, he depicted with great precision the monuments of Paris: Notre-
Dame, the Sainte-Chapelle, the basilica of Saint-Denis.*

NICOLAS FROMENT.—The Raising of Lazarus (1461). Florence,
Uffizi Gallery.

This painting, executed for a Tuscan convent, shows a marked influen[ce]
Rogier van der Weyden adapted to the Provençal harshness of Fromen[t]

MASTER OF MOULINS.—The Nativity of Cardinal Rolin (about 1480).
Detail: The Virgin. Museum of Autun.

softness and harmony typical of the School of the Loire characterize this
ing of the Virgin in which one still finds the influence of the intensified
line of the Flemish School.

Louis Brea (School of Nice).—Pietà.   Nice, Church of Cimiez.

THE MASTER OF MOULINS.—The Virgin in Glory (about 1499). Detail.
Moulins Cathedral.

Compared with the painting on page 109, the triptych of Moulins shows a progress in the sense of harmony which likens this work to the Italian paintings of the same period. The identification of the Master of Moulins with Jean Perréal has become more and more uncertain.

RODRIGO DE OSONA, THE YOUNGER.—St. Dennis (detail). Valencia Cathedr

PAINTING IN SPAIN AND PORTUGAL
UNTIL THE END OF THE 15th CENTURY

WE must not expect to encounter many medieval primitives in Spa
What is to be found in the peninsula belongs chiefly to the reg
of the Pyrenees and Catalonia, which virtually escaped invasion. Ad
rable miniatures are at the root of Spanish painting of the Middle Ages,
at that period the international affiliations of the great religious ord
retarded any national diffusion of its diverse artistic expression. Byzanti
Italian, French and Irish influences exerted themselves either simulta
ously or successively.

There is a Spanish touch in the *Biblia Secunda* of San Isodoro de Le
of 1162; in the Spanish part of the *Biblia de Avila* of the late 12th
early 13th century; and especially in the famous *Apocalypse of Beatus*,
11th century work which was greatly celebrated and which inspired Rom
esque sculpture in the Languedoc.

[112]

PEDRO SERRA.—Altar-piece of the Pentecost (detail). Manresa Cathedral.

BARTOLOME BERMEJO.—The Virgin with Dead Christ.
Barcelona Cathedral.

In Aragon, the former Cathedral of Roda preserves paintings of the sec
half of the 13th century. But it was in Catalonia, thanks to better c
munication with Italy, France and Byzantium, that mural painting produ
works which have been preserved for us in certain churches of the Pyren
The finest of these are doubtless those of the apse of San Clemen de Tal
as well as the mural paintings of San Juan de Bohi (*The Stoning of Step*
and *Juggling Scenes*), the *Baptism of Christ* in Santa Eulalia de Estab
the *Scenes from the Life of St. Nicholas* in Santa Maria de Tarrasa and

intings on panels which were collected in the Museum of Vich. All
ow a tendency to stylization, which was a persistent trait, and a crude
oring based on bright yellows and reds.

The Catalonian Ferrer Bassa was a contemporary of Giotto and came under
influence. The brothers Jaime and Pedro Serra, also Catalonians, who
d about the end of the century, drew their inspiration from Siena. The
me of Lorenzo de Zaragoza, who worked in the early 15th century, denotes
Aragonese origin.

The region of Valencia produced, in the first half of the 15th century, Père
colau and Andrès Marzal de Sax, as well as the great propagator of the
mish influence (although he had not adopted the technique of oil paint-
), Luis Dalmau, who died after 1440. To the second half of the century
ong more properly: the Valencians Jacomart Baço, of Flemish origin; both
drigo de Osonas, father and son; the Catalonians Jaime Huguet; the
rgos, as well as the Aragonese Pedro de Aponte. The latter encroaches
on the 16th century and brings about the transition between Gothic and
naissance art.

The Catalonian School was at this time the great center of attraction for
inters of the peninsula. Bartolomé de Cardenas, the artist whose red hair
used him to be nicknamed Bermejo, came from Cordova, as did, perhaps,
ster Alfonso, as well as their contemporary, Pedro de Cordoba. The
st two, especially the former, are great painters who expressed the auster-
and the tragic sense of the Spanish soul.

Bartolomé Bermejo, born at Cordova about 1440, had passed not only
ough Valencia, a more original and more Spanish province than Catalonia,
t also through Aragon, whose local character was vigorous enough to
duce a Goya.

The genius of Castille began slowly to develop in the 14th century, but
a long time it stood in need of foreign stimulus. Italians, such as
erardo Starnina and Nicholas Florentino, and later Flemings, came to
onize the country artistically, sowing seed of an unexpected flowering.
n 1460, Nuno Gonçalves, who stands comparison with the greatest
sters, painted at Lisbon the *Retable of Saint Vincent*. He was Portuguese,
t at that time the frontier between Spain and Portugal was not overtly
ceptible. Moreover, there were to be Spanish-Portuguese painters at a
er date: Alonzo Sanchez Coello, and the greatest of them all, Diego de
va y Velasquez, whose patronym is Portuguese.

Flemish influence became paramount in Spanish art. There is a strong
k between the Spaniards and the Flemings: it is the love, and the sense,
realism. It may perhaps be said that Flemish influence served to
eguard the independence of Spanish painting, threatened at one time by
overpowering splendor of Italian art.

NUNO GONÇALVES.—Retable of St. Vincent (detail).   Lisbon Museum.

Isolated in the Portuguese School, this masterpiece which represents, group around the Holy Infant, Henry the Navigator, Alfonso V, maritime merchan knights, and notables of Lisbon, remains related to the grand "Burgundia style of Jan van Eyck's art.

CATALONIAN SCHOOL.—The Martyrdom of St. Cugat. Barcelona Museum.

*Formerly ascribed to a certain unidentified "Master Alfonso," this cruel paint-
ing may be due, according to recent findings, to a German master who worked
in Barcelona.*

THE ITALIAN RENAISSANCE IN THE 16th CENTUR

I N the last quarter of the 15th century, a great change was noticeable
the quality of Florentine draughtsmanship. Line lost the hard precisi
which had heretofore characterized it and began to merge with the su
rounding shadows.

A new means of defining forms in space was thus discovered by Leonar
da Vinci. This master was the most complete expression of the Renaissar
—perhaps the most complete of the human spirit, at that period, being at t
same time painter, sculptor, musician, alchemist, architect and engine
For him, painting was a *cosa mentale*, a thing of the mind. It has been sa
that Leonardo lived between two worlds and pursued relentlessly that arc
of investigation which had spurred on his medieval predecessors.
his discovery of chiaroscuro and his intellectual curiosity, he ranks as t
first great modern artist.

The multiplicity of Leonardo's studies and interests in all domains
human knowledge can be seen from his drawings. He first tried to captu
form in all the subtleties of modeling; later he discovered the world
atmosphere, within which modern painting would henceforth unfold.

Having been obliged to flee Milan when the city was captured by t
French, Leonardo entered the service of Caesar Borgia, as architect a
engineer. In 1500, he began in Florence the portrait of *Mona Lisa*, on whi
he worked for four years. It was acquired by Francis I, a great admir
of the artist, who brought Leonardo to France, where he died.

Leonardo da Vinci was a savant as well as a painter. He delved into t
secrets of nature before attempting to reconstitute it. Two preoccupatio
are apparent in his works: to make art the ultimate purpose of science, a
to express through beauty the inner harmony of the world. His paint
works are very few. All suffered from the experiments he made with t
chemical ingredients of color.

Leonardo's influence was great even during his lifetime. He attract
numerous pupils to his Milan studio. Among these, Luini best assimilat
the manner and especially the spirit of his master. Another of Leonard
disciples, Bazzi, better known as Sodoma, renewed the School of Siena.
works are characterized by a decadent charm and a certain languid grac

At the time, Michelangelo was becoming known, Florence was stirred
the fervent exhortations of a Dominican monk named Savonarola. B
although the latter did not hesitate to burn those works which did not confor
with his austere doctrine, he did not condemn art itself. To a certain degr
he even contrived to inspire artists with a high purpose. Several of the
were indelibly impressed by his teachings; Lorenzo di Credi and F

LEONARDO DA VINCI.—Mona Lisa.   Paris, Musée du Louvre.

LEONARDO DA VINCI.—The Annunciation.   Florence, Uffizi Gallery.

This work, which still shows all the characteristics of the Florentine style of
15th century, had long been ascribed to Verrocchio. However, it is now believe
be a work of Leonardo's youth, executed when he was in the studio of Verrocc

Bartolommeo both burnt their profane works and thereafter dedicated the
selves to religious art.   It is said that the sermons of Savonarola w
Michelangelo's favorite reading while working on the Sistine Chapel.

Michelangelo's first master was Ghirlandaio, but he also studied w
great care the frescoes of Masaccio.   The vital power of his genius exten
to various arts: sculpture, architecture, poetry and painting.   He expres
the heroic destiny of man through the athletic strength of the body.
the aspirations, emotions and passions of humanity were for him personi
in the nude, which he nearly always represented in action.   Repose was
him almost an unknown term.   Primarily a sculptor, he was induced by
demands of Pope Julius II to transcend the limitations of his art by paint
the frescoes of the Sistine Chapel at the Vatican.

The frescoes decorating the vaulting of the Sistine Chapel are perhaps
greatest pictorial achievement of all epochs and countries.   Although
had never worked in fresco before, Michelangelo bent this monumen
technique to serve his powerful inspiration.   The method of fresco paint
was moreover in keeping with his sculptural concept of form.   A div
curse seems to blow over all these figures of the Old Testament, twist
their Herculean bodies.   The Prophets and Sibyls convey in their tita
gestures the destiny of all mankind.

Curiously enough, while Michelangelo was enriching the Sistine Cha
with his tumultuous compositions, a very different art was express

LEONARDO DA VINCI.—The Virgin of the Rocks. Paris, Musée du Louvre.

Commissioned in 1483, this painting was probably finished in 1490. The modeled relief, revealing the bone structure of the figures, shows Leonardo's inclination for analysis which he inherited from the Florentine tradition. In Mona Lisa (circa 1500, p. 119), and in St. Anne (circa 1511), on the contrary, he softens the modeling to express beauty and harmony.

RAPHAEL SANZIO.— St. George and the Dragon. Washington, D. C
National Gallery.

The small size of this canvas, which belongs nevertheless to the Florent
School, undoubtedly aided Raphael to recapture the naïvety of his early peri
when he was in the studio of Perugino, at Perugia.

BERNARDINO LUINI.—The Adoration of the Magi. Saronno, Sanctuary.

A student of Leonardo, the Milanese Luini imitated the suavity of his master's
expressions, but did not understand the intellectual principles of his art. In
his scattered compositions, Luini seems to seek only the picturesque.

itself simultaneously in the same Vatican palace. Pope Julius II asked a young painter from Urbino, named Raphael Sanzio, to deco some of the rooms in his private apartments. Although only twenty- years old, Raphael had already realized his talent. He had originally l a pupil of Perugino, from whom he acquired the rather mincing graces of Umbrian School. He then worked in Florence, where Leonardo taught the analytical approach to form. He arrived in Rome—which still ign modern art—rich with the experience of the first Renaissance.

Entrusted by his uncle, the architect Bramante, with the decoratio several rooms of the Vatican, called the Stanze, Raphael began with the known as *The Signature*, in which he represented the great attainm of human knowledge in a series of frescoes. These represent the hig expression of Renaissance humanism, whose dream it was to reco paganism with Christianity. By the balance of his composition and majesty of his figures, Raphael admirably rendered this idea. The soj of Michelangelo in Rome greatly stimulated Raphael's ardor and certa exerted an influence on his talent, perhaps an unfortunate one. Altho he was aided by numerous pupils, often contenting himself with m giving out the sketches and drawings of his compositions, the number importance of the works executed by him during the last years of life is considerable. In the frescoes of the Villa Farnese, devoted to *History of Psyche*, he drew his inspiration from antique painting and prod the first example of the great mythological composition. It is said tha died at the moment Leo X was thinking of naming him Cardinal, w finishing the picture of the *Transfiguration* for the Cathedral of Narbo today in the Vatican.

No two artists could provide greater contrast than Michelangelo Raphael. The former was taciturn and somber, releasing his torme soul in tumultuous compositions of titanic proportion; the latter exert great personal charm on all who approached him. As Vasari has sa Raphael: "that man, who was loved not only of men but of animals de of reason, always caused harmony and a serene joy to reign around h This great artist died at the very height of his precocious genius, in at 37 years of age.

Raphael had grouped around him a brilliant school of artists gene older than himself. Among these, Giulio Romano was the most remark Called to Mantua by Federigo Gonzaga, he proved himself to be a sl architect and engineer, as well as a fine decorator.

Seven years after the death of Raphael, Rome was sacked by the tr of the Connétable de Bourbon; but Venice, escaping from a like destiny victorious over all the leagues formed against her, blossomed with a splendor. The true heirs or creators of classical art were no longer t

RAPHAEL SANZIO.—The Madonna of the Finch. Florence, Uffizi Gallery.

In this Florentine period (1504-1508), Raphael studies the laws of grand style,
composition, harmony, rhythm and beauty. These plastic experiments are
carried out in a series of Madonnas, all of which are executed in pyramid form,
according to strict classical principles.

MICHELANGELO BUONARROTI.—The Creation of Man.   Rome, Sistine Cha
Vatican.

*God imparts the spark of life to man.   This inert figure will shortly arise
display its Herculean physique.*

found in Florence or in Rome, but in Venice, which played a preponde
part in the gradual revolution that led artists to free themselves from
authority of the Church and turn toward the magnificent and limi
domain of feeling.

One of the greatest painters of this school, Giorgione, inaugurated a
method founded on the symphonic relationship of colors, with drav
demoted from the prime role accorded it by Florence—and still respe
by Michelangelo and Raphael.   For Giorgione, heir to the sensitivit
Giovanni Bellini, landscape was no longer mere background scenery
invaded the whole canvas, enveloping the figures with its atmosph
Giorgione also developed a subject which painting has never exhausted:
glorification of female beauty in a setting of the beauty of nature.

Titian was, at first, a faithful disciple of Giovanni Bellini, in whose st
he met Giorgione, who exerted a very real influence over him.   Titian e
discovered and celebrated the intimate communion existing between i
and nature, and was truly one of the heralds of Romanticism.   He peo
his landscapes with superb, voluptuous nudes; he was the first of the
versal painters.   Equally expert in depicting the pure beauty of a Mado
the voluptuousness of Venus or the sufferings of Christ, he has expre
the whole range of human sentiment.   He was also a magnificent portrai

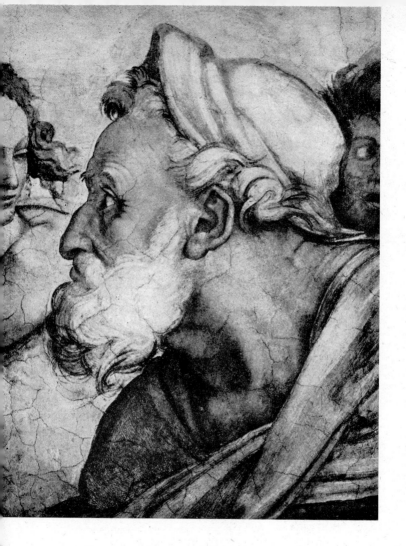

MICHELANGELO BUONARROTI.—The Prophet Ezekiel (detail). Rome, Sistine Chapel, Vatican.

...is prophets of superhuman stature, Michelangelo has expressed the different ...ects of inspiration. He has given to Ezekiel his own facial characteristics.

ANDREA DEL SARTO.—St. John the Baptist.   Florence, Pitti Gallery

Deprived by Rome and Milan of its greatest masters, the Florentine School
the 16th century becomes sterile: the line becomes more and more brittle,
the modeling less firm; the bodies seem flaccid and lifeless.

RAPHAEL SANZIO.—The School of Athens (detail). Rome, Palace of the Vatican. Stanza della Segnatura. *The frescoes are one of the most beautiful expressions of the marriage of thought and art. The balance of the compositions expresses the wisdom of the ancients and the truth of the Faith. The architecture of the School of Athens was inspired from the St. Peter's of Bramante.*

MICHELANGELO BUONARROTI.—The Holy Family (detail).
About 1503-1506.   Florence, Uffizi Gallery.

With its muscular female figure and its richly modeled draperies, this paint
already contains the essence of the monumental and superhuman art of
Sistine Chapel.

can be seen in the Florence galleries. In Titian, all the qualities of the netian School were combined. He died at the age of ninety-nine, honor-by the whole of Europe and laden with distinctions by Charles V and ilip II.

Among the artists who studied in Titian's atelier, one, Tintoretto, had ambition of surpassing his master by combining, as he said, "the ughtsmanship of Michelangelo and the color of Titian." He was as tor-nted as Michelangelo by the drama of humanity. His figures, move dlessly in a twilight pierced with lightning. The serene and fleshy Vene-n School ends with this dramatist who heralds Baroque painting by his se of space interest and contorted bodies. His principal work is the coration of the Scuola San Rocco, which represents the New Testament.

Veronese shared with Titian the honor of being one of the masters of the netian School, and one of the greatest Italian decorators. He was drawn vast compositions and excelled at disposing in his contrasts and combi-ions of coloring, placing his figures in their gorgeous draperies against oosing architectural backgrounds. Veronese was the last great Venetian ster.

t is hardly possible to speak of a "School" of Parma, which is represented only one artist of importance: Correggio, whose influence on the last lian masters, the Bolognese and through them on the whole of European was, however, considerable.

Although he spent his short life in his little native town of Parma, rreggio greatly expanded the universe of art. His was a truly original rit who imitated no one. He was the first in Italy to conquer a sense space, an art later developed by the Baroque masters, and he decorated first two domes ever painted in ceiling perspective. He was the first to nonstrate that the most powerful effects could be produced by analogy vell as by opposition. No one has known better than he how to blend his ires into the surrounding atmosphere and light. His types of women l tenderly smiling children were imitated until the 18th century; his refin-profane style was an early prelude to Baroque æsthetics.

However, his greatest works are frescoes. No one has ever surpassed a in the decoration of domed ceilings. That of San Giovanni of Parma uld no doubt be the finest work of this kind ever painted, had he not passed himself in the cupola of *The Assumption* of the Cathedral of rma.

The great movement of the Renaissance ended in Italy with a form of thetics known as Mannerism. This is a stylistic extreme that affected ists challenged by the example of the great masters, leading them to ggerate the "manner" of the latter by elongating proportions, contorting itudes and giving affected expressions to the features. Each school

CORREGGIO.—St. Bernard.   Cathedral of Parma (detail of the Dome)

was to leave behind it a wake of Mannerists: in Florence, Bronzino, Salvi followers of 15th century art, Pontormo, Vasari, Il Rosso, imitators Michelangelo; in Parma, Il Parmegianino who exaggerated the effects Correggio; in Rome, Giulio Romano who inherited Raphael's later man influenced by Michelangelo.   Mannerism was to exert a great influence European art, for it became predominant in all Italy, except Venice, fr 1530 onwards.

PONTORMO.—The Descent from the Cross.   Florence, Church of St. Felicity.

The influence of Michelangelo, even during the lifetime of the great artist,
finally exhausted the resources of Florentine art, imposing upon the painters
a feeling of futility and revolt which produced that strange and troubled style
called Mannerism.

TITIAN.—Portrait of Pope Paul III.   Naples, National Museum.

With more humanism, and no less penetration than Bronzino, Titian kn̄
how to render the inner spirit of the person who posed before him.   Here,
unfortunate Pope, Paul III, appears anxious and worried.

BRONZINO.—Portrait of Lucrezia Panciatichi.   Florence, Uffizi Gallery.

*Though only a mediocre painter of religious and mythological subjects, the
Florentine Bronzino produced some of the most striking and stately portraits
of the 16th century.*

TITIAN.—Madonna and Child with St. John and St. Catherine. London, National Gallery.

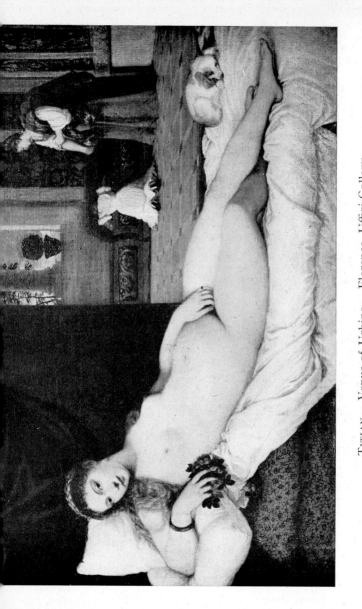

TITIAN.—Venus of Urbino. Florence, Uffizi Gallery

Executed for the Duke of Urbino, this picture may be considered as painting's first "académie" (study from a nude). Giorgione's Venus, which preceded it, was still a goddess; here Venus is a mortal.

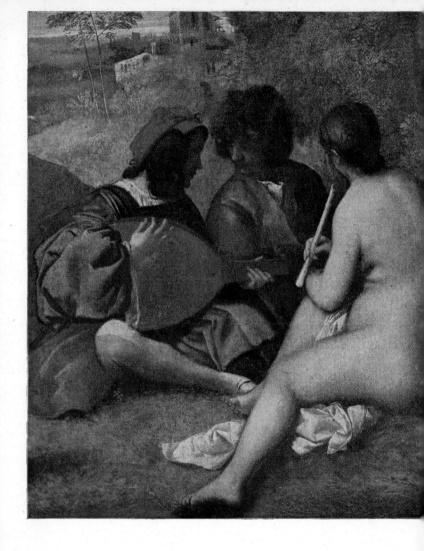

GIORGIONE.—Concert in the Open Air. Paris, Musée du Louvre.

*A fellow student of Titian in the studio of Giovanni Bellini, Giorgione is
first artist to produce an intimate relationship between figures and landsca
the "Concert in the Open Air" is like the symbol of this unity.*

GIORGIONE.—The Tempest.   Venice, Academy of Fine Arts.

*importance of the landscape appears clearly in this work ; the figures seem
ewhat superfluous, and their absence would in no way spoil the composition.*

VERONESE. — The Family of Darius before Alexander. London, National Gallery.

Little concerned with expression or feeling, as was Titian, Veronese indulged in the pure pleasure of composing beautifully decorative and rhythmic canvases, with princely figures, in a magnificent architectural setting.

TINTORETTO.—Bacchus and Ariadne Crowned by Venus.   Venice, Du
Palace.

The last great painter of Venice, Tintoretto is, in a way, its Michelan;
He heralds Baroque art by his sense of composition in space.   Here, his fig
seem to float in the air.

RAPHAEL SANZIO.—Dona Velata (about 1514). Florence, Pitti Palace.

Dona Velata, which belongs to the Roman period of Raphael, well reflects the feeling of majesty that he derived from his contact with antiquity.

ANTOINE CARON.—The Sibyl of Tibur.   Paris, Musée du Louvre.

The fanciful monuments through which Antoine Caron pictured Roman an-
quity were inspired by the temporary constructions erected for celebration
which Caron often participated as a decorator.

THE SCHOOL OF FONTAINEBLEAU

FAVORED by the wars of Italy, the Italian Renaissance initiated
conquest of Gothic France.   In 1508, the Cardinal of Amboise had
Chapel of Gaillon painted by Andrea Solario.   In 1513, a company
Bolognese decorated with frescoes the vaulting of the Cathedral of Albi.

It was, however, only in 1530, a decisive date in the history of the Fre
Renaissance, that Italianism won the day.   With its mythological galle
decorated with frescoes and stucco, the Château of Fontainebleau, a hun
resort for which François I forsook Chambord and the Valley of the L
attracted Il Rosso in 1531 and Primaticcio in 1532.   Like Avignon in

FRANÇOIS CLOUET.—Diane of Poitiers in Her Bath. Richmond, England.
Cook Collection.

François Clouet has idealized the face of the King's mistress to give it the regular-
and modeled relief of ancient statuary. He takes his inspiration from the
na Lisa, which had been in the royal collection since the time of Francis I.

SCHOOL OF FONTAINEBLEAU.—Portrait of a Woman. George Wildenst
Collection. — *Many are the anonymous painters who have evoked femin
beauty with a purity of countenance and with smooth, lithe, undulating bod*

ne, Fontainebleau became "a second Rome," whence the Italian Renais-
ance spread not only to France, but also to the whole of Northern Europe.
The influence of the Bolognese Primaticcio, as well as his preference for
ngated forms, is to be found again in the religious or mythological works
the French historical painters of the 16th century; from Jean Cousin
e Elder down to Antoine Caron and Martin Fréminet.   Like several other
ench painters of the 16th century, for instance Antoine Caron and Fran-
s Quenel, Jean Cousin was called upon to design tapestry cartoons.

The need to flatter the mistress of Henri II, the châtelaine of Anet, led to
abundance of mythological pictures, representing Diana as huntress or
her.

Mythological portraits appear as early as the 16th century in the en-
els of Léonard Limosin, who disguised Catherine de Medici as Ceres
d Henri III as Apollo.   This tradition of antiquity was maintained by
toine Caron of Beauvais, painter of Roman pageantry, who was appointed
the court of Catherine de Medici.

Under Henri IV, the School of Fontainebleau entered into a second phase,
ebted to the influx of painters from the Netherlands.   Ambroise Dubois
Antwerp, Jean and Nicholas van Hoey, descendants of Lucas van
yden, are the chief representatives of this group.

Of great historical interest, since its influence extended over the whole
Europe and far into the 17th century and included the Lothavingian
ques Bellange as well as the Norman, Nicholas Poussin, the School of
ntainebleau was merely a hothouse of the Italian Renaissance.

t was in portrait painting that the French School of the 16th century
wed its greatest originality.   Its contribution consisted chiefly in the
eralized use of pencil (or "créon") drawings, lightly enhanced with pastel,
ich served as preparation and model for the final painted portrait.

The same may be said of Clouet's pencil drawings as of La Tour's pastel
liminaries: these direct observations sketched from life are generally more
uitive than the final portraits, overfinished at the studio.   On the other
d, Clouet's portraits in oil have something linear and graphic which
rays their origin; they are more drawn than painted.   His son François,
the contrary, worked in a more fluid manner.

The masters of the style are in fact the Clouets, Jean and François, who
often mistaken one for the other on account of their surname; both were
ed Janet, and François Clouet signed "Franciscus Janetius."   That
n was of foreign origin is certain, but that he came from Flanders is mere
othesis.   All French portraits of the 16th century were once indiscrimin-
ly attributed to him, at least those of a certain size, the smaller ones
ng given to Corneille de Lyon.

he surname of Clouet's rival, Corneille de Lyon, might lead one to

JEAN CLOUET.—Portrait of Francis I (detail). Paris, Musée du Louv

The perception of Jean Clouet, which is more analytical than that of his
François, serves to portray the features of his model with all their inte
individuality; François, on the contrary, tends to idealize them.

[148]

ppose that he was French by birth.
e was actually born in Holland, but
me to France when young and settled
Lyons, where he became naturalized
1547. To him are generously attri-
ted all the little portraits painted
wood with a miniature touch over
bluish or water-green background.
e very unequal quality of these
y pictures proves that many are
dio replicas or perhaps the works of
son, who was also named Corneille;
that there are supposed to be two
rneilles de Lyon just as there are
o Jean Cousins and two Clouets.
It is worthy of note that, unlike the
ouets, Corneille worked without the
l of black-lead preparations. No
ncil drawing by him is known.
Beside these paintings on wood,
e art of the Valois Court produced
e magnificent enamel portraits of
onard Limosin, in which the imitation
the Italian masters who influenced
e Fontainebleau School is allied to
at of the Clouets.

FRENCH SCHOOL, 16th CENTURY.—
Portrait of Elizabeth of Austria,
Queen of France. Paris, Musée
du Louvre.

The last representatives of the art of portrait painting during the reigns
Henri III and Henri IV have left us few works beside pencil sketches.
ese artists were Jean Decourt of Limoges, who began as a painter on
amel and succeeded François Clouet, the dynasties of Dumonstier and
esnel and, finally, Pierre Lagneau.

Etienne Dumonstier, or Dumontier, was sent to Vienna by Catherine de
dici. A portrait of a woman in a green, slashed dress at the Louvre, is
ributed to him. His brother Pierre has left us a fine, full-length portrait
Sully, Henri IV's prime minister. The dynasty continued with Pierre,
nephew, and his cousin Daniel.

As for the Quesnel brothers, François and Nicholas, they were the sons
Pierre Quesnel, painter to James V, King of Scotland, at Edinburgh.

Pierre Lagneau's reinforced pencil studies, mark the end of the evol-
on of this charming art which became extinct at the end of the reign
Henri IV, to revive much later, in another form, with Robert Nanteuil
d La Tour.

GERMAN ART IN THE 16th CENTURY

AT the beginning of the 16th century, the reign of the German empe: Maximilian saw the outbreak of religious struggles. Maximilia successor, Charles V, strove to hold together the vast domains he h conquered in spite of war with France, insurrection of peasants and nob and incessant religious conflict. German art reflects the torment of a peo always on the watch.

Albrecht Dürer was the most original and powerful representative German art in the 16th century. Born in 1471, he studied, as we ha already seen, in Wolgemut's studio at a moment when the School of Nure berg was acquiring more realism and energy under Dutch influence. Hav ended his apprenticeship, Dürer traveled during four years. At Colmar, acquired Schongauer's tradition of etching; a journey to Venice, where came in contact with Giovanni Bellini, completed his training. Indeed, jealousy that foreign artists generally bore him, and of which he bitte complained, would seem a proof of the outstanding reputation he had alrea acquired abroad. Yet Giovanni Bellini had a real friendship for Dür

In the wide scope of his intellectual interests, Albrecht Dürer recá Leonardo da Vinci. Like the latter, he was interested by engineering p blems. He drew up one of the first treatises on fortifications follow the invention of gunpowder. It is curious to note that in this treatise shows great skill in creating and arranging shelters in which beleague: populations could resist the fire of the enemy.

However, it is undeniable that Dürer's art remained distinctly hostile classical beauty, in spite of the fact that he visited Italy twice and ev made two prolonged stays at Venice, where he transmitted many new id on draughtsmanship to the pupils of the Bellinis. But, once back in native town of Nuremberg, Dürer showed that he had gained nothing fr them, and that Latin harmony exerted little or no influence on him. his life, he was possessed by the Germanic genius of analysis.

In Germany, he received many orders from the Emperor Maximili Dürer was an ardent partisan of the Reformation and knew Luth Melanchthon and Zwingli.

He painted a great number of pictures, somewhat sharp of coloring a trenchant of design; his finest and most expressive works perhaps are etchings and his pen-and-ink drawings from nature. He used to say: '

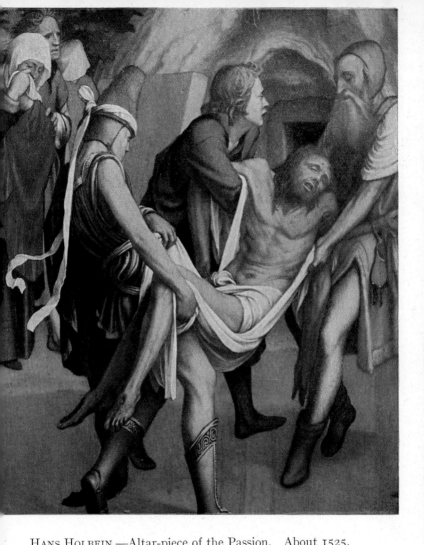

HANS HOLBEIN.—Altar-piece of the Passion.   About 1525.
The Entombment (detail).   Basel, Museum of Fine Arts.

religious subjects, where his imagination finds itself somewhat restrained,
ns Holbein follows more closely the general style of the period and shows
perhaps less originality.

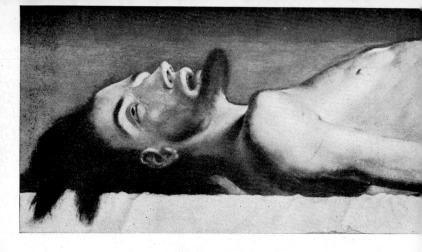

HANS HOLBEIN.—The Entombment. 1521 (detail). Basel,
Museum of Fine Arts.

Nowhere else, perhaps, as in this dead body with its gaunt eyes, emaciated fa
and greenish flesh tints, has Holbein affirmed so intensely his concern for luc
objectivity which sometimes takes on an aspect of cruelty.

reality, art resides in nature; he who can extract it, possesses it." B
Dürer was, above all, an engraver. He was, with Mantegna, the creator
modern engraving. He practised wood engraving with the assistance
his pupils, but his finest works are the tool etchings on which he worke
alone. In *The Great Fortune, The Knight, Death and the Devil,* ar
Melancolia, he expressed in the guise of philosophical allegory the bas
pessimism of Germanic thought.

In the midst of the far-reaching effects of the Italian Renaissance, Dür
remained a Gothic. Nothing hindered the intense realism of his expressio
He is, beyond question, the greatest German artist of the Middle Age
possessing the sensibility and archaic brutality of the primitives, whi
having nevertheless acquired a taste for the universal, which was the gre
quest of the Renaissance.

In 1520, Dürer went to Holland, where he received a triumphal welcon
He was able to make an exhaustive study of the Flemish masters, to who
realism and precision he was greatly drawn.

At Augsburg, Hans Holbein the Elder submitted to the influence
Giovanni Bellini, but his fame was soon surpassed by that of his son, Ha

bein the Younger. The latter, although born in Augsburg, was a true
nopolitan. He settled first at Basel, where he became the friend of
smus, of whom he painted a magnificent portrait. Then he went to
:land, where he enjoyed the favor of Henry VIII. No other German
iter can compare with him for his vigorous yet warm color. His
;ious paintings give but a poor idea of his talent; he was pre-eminently
ortraitist. Before executing a portrait, Holbein was in the habit of
ving a "preparation" either in sepia or in pencil. The Basel Museum
:esses a magnificent collection of these. While in England, which
bein visited on the invitation of Sir Thomas More, he painted the
raits of the highest dignitaries of the realm.

ALBRECHT DÜRER.—Portrait of himself (detail).　1493.　Paris,
Musée du Louvre.

*omparison between these two portraits of Albrecht Dürer, painted some
's apart, shows the progress of the spirit of the Renaissance in the artist's
*. The first is a true likeness, humble and tormented, the second an
lized portrait in which the artist has taken on the face of Christ himself.*

ALBRECHT ALTDORFER.—The Battle of Arbela (detail). 1529. Mun
Pinakothek.

Altdorfer's Battle of Arbela *is a universe where, in a limited space, one obse
the clash of armed multitudes in a grandiose setting of mountains, sea,
sky—an expression of the cosmic feeling peculiar to the Germans.*

Holbein's portraits occupy a very special place in the history of Ger
art. He was the first artist since Van Dyck to depict absolute since
and truth. He knew how to place his models in noble and elegant attitu
to clothe and suggest their forms without encumbering them. His alv
discreet and subtle color envelops the form in delicate nuances.

Lucas Cranach, a follower of Dürer, was the first truly Protestant pai
He passed his life in Saxony, where he founded a school which, howe
did not survive him. Cranach was far from equaling Dürer or Holbein.
worked hard, but his pictures are very uneven, although he had a cer
originality. He was particularly interested in the nude and in sub
borrowed from pagan mythology, and he painted several figures of A

ALBRECHT ALTDORFER.　The Nativity.　Berlin, German Museum.

*fanciful imagination of Altdorfer excels in evoking dawn, dusk and the
~ries of the night, pierced by fulgurating gleams of light and enhanced by
ritions in the clouds.　He is one of the artists who has best suggested the
~ of the supernatural by means of the strangest aspects of the natural world.*

HANS FRIES.—The Martyrdom of St. Barbara.   Swabia, Museum of Freib
Hans Fries, who belonged to the Swiss School, was one of the German ar
most frequently inspired by strange visions and scenes of martyrdom

LUCAS CRANACH. St. Jerome. 1502. Vienna, Museum.

*he work of Lucas Cranach, Nature is always the prime mover of all things:
man and animals seem to mingle with the trees and clouds in this
mysterious world of the Germanic forest.*

Lucas Cranach.—Venus.   New York, Otto H. Kahn Collection.

The influence of antiquity in Cranach's work produced delicate mytholo,
figures which, by their contorted posture, retain certain characteristics o,
tormented style of Gothic art.

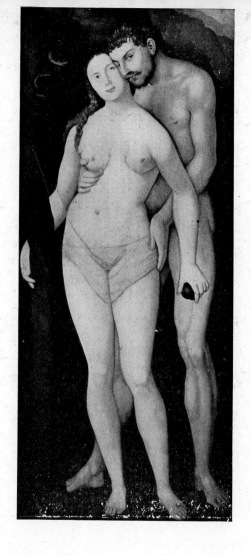

S Baldung Grien. Adam and Eve.   Bonn, Kunsthistorisches Institut.

*nudes of Hans Baldung Grien are closer to the Italian style and denote a
better-assimilated ancient influence; they are, however, less graceful.*

HANS HOLBEIN. Jane Seymour (detail). Vienna, Kunsthistorisches Mus

MATHIAS GRÜNEWALD.—Altar-piece of Isenheim. About 1510.
The hands of the Magdalen (detail). Colmar, Unterlinden Museum.

e hands of the Magdalen in the Crucifixion, with their fingers clenched in
'n supplication, are like the symbol of the deep torment which animated
German art in the 16th century.

HANS HOLBEIN.—Portrait of the Astronomer Nicolas Kratzer.
Paris, Musée du Louvre.

*Hans Holbein's lucid power of observation excels in portraying the thought,
countenance, the cold character and the exacting spirit of this man of scien*

ULRICH APT THE ELDER.—The Adoration of the Magi (detail).
Paris, Musée du Louvre.

d Eve. But, curiously enough, he was profoundly opposed both in
nception and style to antique art; to an even greater extent than Dürer,
: remained faithful to the Gothic. He ranked high as a portrait painter
d knew how to render admirably both the vigor and the bestiality of the
xons, his contemporaries.

On the Danube, a few lesser masters such as Albrecht Altdorfer and Wolf
uber were interested chiefly in landscape. Altdorfer was a more gifted
lorist than Dürer and his compositions were of a fantastic nature. His
ttle of Arbela is one of the finest works of the 16th century.

The greatest painter of the period in Germany is Mathias Grünewald, who
orked on the Middle Rhine and in Alsace. His daring feats of coloring
e equal to those of the greatest Venetian masters. In the Isenheim
etable at the Museum of Colmar, which contains a sanguinary Crucifixion,
: has expressed in dramatic style the pessimism of 16th century Germany
which Dürer gave a philosophical tone.

THE RENAISSANCE IN THE LOW COUNTRIES

At the end of the 15th century, Antwerp took the place of Bruges as th
center of Flemish art, the latter city falling into decay as its port wa
invaded by silt. A bustling town, Antwerp in the 16th century was a ma
seat of Humanism and the magnetic pole of the Renaissance in Norther
Europe. At an early date, contact with Italy was established, as is prove
by the art of Quentin Massys, whose reputation was great and who wa
much admired by Dürer and Holbein. In his triptych of the *Holy Kinshi*
painted in 1509, Massys shows that he was not insensitive to the art
Leonardo da Vinci. During Massys' lifetime, Patinir took a step forwar
in landscape by painting, for the first time, pictures with nature as the
sole object, or in which the subject or pretext *(The Rest on the Flight in
Egypt)* is merely incidental.

In the meantime, Bruges gave Flemish art another great artist.
contemporary of Massys, Gerard David was less aware of the new influence
he continued the serene style of Memlinc, with less mysticism but great
firmness.

Until the end of the 16th century Antwerp was an exceedingly lively cent
where artists from all regions met. The cities of the Northern Netherland
Haarlem, Utrecht, Leyden, were also very active, the interchange of artis
sometimes making it difficult to distinguish between schools. Thus Ja
Gossart, known as Mabuse, born at Maubeuge, worked at Mechlin an
Utrecht. He made a trip to Italy and brought back to Flanders the influen
of Mantegna; he was the first and even the only Flemish painter exclusive
interested in the human body dissociated from nature, in the manner of th
15th century Italians.

Lucas van Leyden (1494-1533), a contemporary of Massys, was pr
occupied by questions of a technical order, above all in his early works, su
as *Abigail* and *The Resurrection of Lazarus*. He was particularly celebrat
as an engraver, and Vasari goes so far as to consider him Dürer's superio
Lucas was only twelve years old when he painted a picture of Saint Hube
which provoked the admiration and astonishment of his contemporari
His best-known work, apart from his innumerable and remarkable engravin
is the triptych of the *Last Judgment*, at Leyden. There is a deep torment
this work which evokes that of the Italian Mannerists, and which affect
more or less the whole of Europe in the 16th century. The art of Mart
van Heemskerk of Haarlem was still more morbid.

GÉRARD DAVID.—The Baptism of Christ. 1507. Bruges, Communal Museum.—*Gérard David prolongs until the beginning of the 16th century the Flemish art of the Gothic period, and particularly the tradition of Memlinc which he took in at Bruges. But in David's work the spirit of the Renaissance is displayed by attention to plastic problems and a keen sensibility to landscape.*

JAN GOSSART.—Portrait of Jean Carondelet. 1517. Paris, Musée du Louv

QUENTIN MASSYS.—The Virgin. 1529. Paris, Musée du Louvre.

QUENTIN MASSYS.—The Banker and his Wife (detail). Paris, Musée Louvre.—*One of the first secular pictures in the painting of the North, this w gives Massys the opportunity of portraying a couple in an interior. Sligh outdated for its time, the picture is, by its objectivity, so close to Jan Van E that it was thought to have been inspired by a lost Van Eyck original. The mir which reflects the street, is a technique borrowed from the Van Eyck traditi*

GÉRARD DAVID.—The Rest on the Flight into Egypt. New York, Bache Collection, Metropolitan Museum of Art.

JAN GOSSART.—Venus and Cupid. 1521.   Paris, A. Schloss Collecti

One of the first mythological paintings of the Low Countries.   The mu.
nude, as well as the classical architecture, reveals an influence o
Renaissance which the artist probably derived directly from Italy.

TIN MASSYS.—Portrait of Peter Giles.   About 1517.   Longford Castle,
Salisbury,   Radnor Collection.

*work is typical of the portraits of the Humanist as the Northern painters
to represent him, seated at his table and surrounded by his books.   The
ss of Peter Giles, secretary of the city of Antwerp, formerly complemented
trait of Erasmus (today in Rome, at the Corsini Palace) ; this diptych
had been painted for a third humanist, Thomas More, of London.*

PIETER AERTSEN.—Kitchen Scene. Amsterdam.

Pieter Aertsen, of Antwerp, painted many rustic and kitchen scenes; but
are in his style certain elements of Italianism which he probably derived
Venice, particularly from the Bassanos. (Note the elegance of his peasa
In the foreground, he likes to display heaps of food. The still-lifes of Fy
Snyders, in the 17th century, spring from these paintings by Aertse

In the second half of the 16th century, artists of the Netherlands emig
to Italy to study in the ateliers of Rome. When they returned to their
country, they produced a hybrid style in which Gothic tradition is ble
with the Transalpine influence. While Jan Mostaert remained closer t
ancestral art, Van Scorel and Van Orley strove in vain to assin
the art of the Renaissance. Antonio Moro, of Utrecht, invited by
Courts of England and Spain, was the greatest portraitist in the
century Netherlands and exerted an influence on the development of Sp
portrait painting.

✓ It was Peter Brueghel the Elder, however, who created the new style.
also studied Italian art, but remained faithful to his Flemish heredity.
was quick to free himself from influences—that of Hieronymus Bosch
that of the Italians. His paintings and compositions describing his cor
poraries were naturalistic rather than religious. He painted the lives c
common folk who lived in the Flemish villages of the 16th century; i
hands art became deliberately profane. Brueghel is considered by 1
as the greatest landscapist of all time; his views are seen in panor
perspective, from a high point which embraces an immense extent of
and water in all their forms: valley, river, mountain, ocean. He

BRUEGHEL THE ELDER.—The Peasant Wedding. Vienna, Museum.

hough he traveled in Italy and may have retained certain principles from trip, Pieter Brueghel did not keep either the style or the manner of the lians. Unlike Pieter Aertsen, his rustic art is entirely indigenous, and his stocky figures are authentic Flemish peasants.

nted the different seasons, and his work is an encyclopædia of nature. n the last third of the 16th century, painters with a preference for chen scenes, such as Pieter Aertsen and Joaquim Beuckelaer, inaugurated paths that were to be followed by the great still-life painters of the next tury. The school ended rather inadequately with a poor imitator of helangelo, Frans Floris. But already in the ateliers of Otho Veen and n Noort, Rubens was preparing the great flowering of the 17th century.

BERNARD VAN ORLEY.—The Altar-piece of the Holy Cross. 1515.
Christ Falling under the Cross. Brussels, Royal Museums.

An eclectic painter, Bernard Van Orley, reflects all the aspects of the past a
present. Certain paintings of his remain Gothic in spirit; in others
imitates Dürer; and for his last works he finds his inspiration in Raph
All these influences converge in a troubled art, with feverish compositions a
contorted figures, which shows all the characteristics of that tormented st
called mannerism.

os Van Cleve.—The Holy Family with St. Anne (detail: St. Anne).
Brussels, Museum.

*art of Joos Van Cleve (formerly called the Master of the Death of Mary) is
to that of Massys, but it has a shade of elegance and tenderness which the
artist may well owe to a sojourn in Cologne.*

JOACHIM PATINIR.—The Rest on the Flight into Egypt. Madrid, Museum of the Prado.

In the 16th century, Patinir is the initiator of the "universal" landscape which depicts, on a vast sweep of

BRUEGHEL THE ELDER.—The Census at Bethlehem. Brussels, Museum.

To the fragmented landscapes of Patinir, Brueghel adds unity. He shows man closely allied with Nature, in keeping with the rhythm of the seasons. His works, of medium dimensions, are like segments of the universe crawling with strenuous life.

Jan Mostaert.—Portrait of Joost Van Bronekhorst.   Paris, Petit Pal

Jan Mostaert painted in his native city of Haarlem and in Brussels for
Court of Margaret of Austria.   His religious compositions are commonpl
but the aristocratic elegance of his portraits is striking.

LUCAS VAN LEYDEN.—Lot and his Daughters. About 1509. Paris, Musée du Louvre.

*cas Van Leyden, a painter of the Northern Low Countries, gives evidence
an imagination inclined toward the strange, and even the fantastic.   He is
thus more closely related to the German painters than to the Flemish.*

BRUEGHEL THE ELDER.—Head of an Old Peasant Woman. Munich, Pinakothek.

In this head of an old peasant woman, Brueghel betrays his sources. T caricatural aspect of the face shows that he developed his art by examining t satirical works of Jerome Bosch.

BRUEGHEL THE ELDER.—The Harvesters (detail). New York, Metropolitan Museum. *No other painter has ever succeeded in expressing as gracefully as Brueghel the intimacy of man and Nature which is peculiar to life in the country. Under snow or sultry heat, harvest time or winter time, a grandiose Nature unalterably dominates man, who seems to be her servant.*

ANTONIO MORO.—Queen Mary of England.   Madrid, Museum of the Prad

A native of Utrecht, and painter to the courts of Brussels, London and Madr
Antonis Mor (changed to Antonio Moro, in Spain) left an unforgetta
gallery of portraits of the rulers of his troubled time.

ANNIBALE CARRACCI.—The Sleep of Venus.   Chantilly, Musée Condé.

...is effort to unite the qualities of the greatest masters, Raphael, Titian and ...helangelo, Annibale Carracci attains only a commonplace art lacking in character.

ART IN ITALY
IN THE 17th AND 18th CENTURIES

...the 17th century, two great tendencies sought to dominate art in Italy. ...With the exception of Venice, which led a completely independent ...lectual life.   The Eclectics strove to assimilate and combine the quali- ...of the great masters of the 16th century, while the Naturalists sought ...iration only in reality.

...s early as the end of the 16th century, the Bolognese School endeavored ...reate a style common to all Italy, formed of the finest elements derived ...n the greatest masters.   These efforts were due largely to the initiative ...odovico Carracci and of his two cousins Agostino and Annibale Carracci. ...y founded their celebrated Academy in 1589 in their native town ...ch was, and still is, the seat of a famous University.   They were in part ...onsible for what was later known as Academism—that is an art based

GUIDO RENI.—Ecce Homo. Paris, Musée du Louvre.

Often reproduced, this devotional picture shows to what degree of insipi̇a
the official religious art of the 17th century had descended.

on formula. They taught that one should borrow from Michelangel￼
magnificent dynamism, from Correggio his pure style, from Raphae
harmonious, symmetrical composition and from the Venetians the a￼
movement and color. Annibale Carracci in particular is known fo￼
fine mythological decoration of the Farnese Palace at Rome, inspired ￼

ꜰʀᴄɪɴᴏ.—The Funeral of St. Petronilla. 1621. Rome, Picture Gallery of the Capitol.

ꜰed under the Carracci's academic discipline, Guercino broke away by
ng, like Caravaggio, to wholesome, rustic human elements, and to an art
' great dramatic effect ordered by the distribution of light and shadow.

Michelangelo and imitated throughout Europe. Carracci's pupils, G
Reni, Guercino and Domenichino, formed the academic art of the
century.

At this period Naturalism, or painting directly from nature, opposed
Academism of the Carracci. The head of this naturalistic school
Michelangelo da Caravaggio, who was as temperamental and brutal in
work as in his life. Wishing to regenerate by Naturalism the art of his
which was stifled by Academism, he introduced the habit of pain
directly from the model, as the masters of the Flemish school had done
so long. The artist sought primarily to create a robust effect, wheth
still-life or in large religious compositions.

Dramatic effects he obtained by means of chiaroscuro, that is, t
violent contrast between shadows and lights, a contrast found onl
cellars or under artificial lighting. Caravaggio's intense realism, so diffe
from the mawkishness then in vogue, was to have considerable conseque
in the whole of Europe. Rubens, Rembrandt, Ribera and Zurbaran ow
him their vigorous sense of reality. His discovery of chiaroscuro effects
to inspire painters of all schools. But the most fervent of his disciples
in Holland.

While Rome endeavored, with artists such as Guercino, to strike a bal
between Academism and the manner of Caravaggio, the schools of Na
Genoa and Milan, exploiting all the resources of chiaroscuro, conceiv
romantic style of painting in which dramatic scenes unfolded themselv
an atmosphere of nocturnes and twilights. At Genoa, visited by Ru
and Van Dyck, Strozzi profited from these theories, while Magnasco in
18th century depicted satirical subjects in an electrical atmosphere. St
and Magnasco, by their satirical romanticism, already herald Goya.
Milan, the overtones of Giuseppe Maria Crespi were more religiou
Naples, Salvator Rosa developed a virtuoso art smacking of charla
ism. Through Naples where he lived, Caravaggio was to exert a st
influence over the destinies of the Spanish School in the 17th century.

Venice, however, manifested the same independence during the
period of her splendor as during her golden age. The slumbering pair
of the 17th century ended in the 18th in an apotheosis of light.

Canaletto and his pupil Guardi were the ideal portraitists of their be
ful native city, while Pietro Longhi was a particularly interesting reco
of Venetian life and customs. The easel pieces and the decorative pain
of Piazzetta have a very modern boldness of composition. Giovanni Bat
Tiepolo, the last great Italian painter, resumed the large decorations de
the Italian School, with a coloring less powerful but more luminous
that of his predecessors.

CARAVAGGIO.—The Crucifixion of St. Peter. 1600-1601. Rome, Church of St. Mary of the People.

CANALETTO.—The Grand Canal and Santa Maria della Salute. Paris, Musée du Louvre.

Canaletto, who worked not only for Venic h t Chi t f E th t ht t d l d

TIEPOLO.—The Finding of the Cross. Venice, Academy. Italian art ends in the apotheosis of Tiepolo. The Baroque feeling is expressed in his work through vast ceiling compositions where the figures seem to float in space.

PIAZZETTA.—Head of a Woman. Nantes, Museum.

Ncesco Guardi.—View of Venice. Paris, Museum André Jacquemart.

*ike Canaletto, the other portraitist of the city of Venice, Guardi, bends his
ts toward rendering the multiple nuances of the light and atmosphere of
his native city.*

RUBENS.—Rubens and Isabel Brandt. 1609-1610. Munich, Pinakotl

Made famous at an early date by his first masterpieces, Rubens, at th
depicts himself, happy, beaming and healthy, in the company of his yo
wife, Isabel Brandt, whom he married in 1609.

PAUL BRIL.—The Creation of the Animals. Rome, Doria Gallery.

hese landscapes, painted at Rome, Paul Bril still shows the picturesque and
'ytical spirit of the 16th century, and at the same time makes a first attempt
at imposing a classical arrangement upon Nature.

FLEMISH ART IN THE 17th CENTURY

URING the 16th century, Flanders had endured fearful tribulations.
When Protestantism spread through the Low Countries, Philip II and
cruel Duke of Alba resolved to stamp it out by means of sanguinary
ession. The Northern Provinces, after a dogged resistance, succeeded
berating themselves from Spanish rule and formed a Republic. Thus
and was constituted. The Southern Provinces, consisting of Flanders
the Walloon country, submitted to their Spanish masters, and Roman
1olicism triumphed. Not counting those who died by the axe or
ugh misery and famine, 60,000 families, including that of Rubens,
grated to Antwerp. Desolation reigned everywhere.

7hen the Low Countries were presented as a marriage portion to the
nta Isabella Claire Eugenia, who married the Archduke Albert of
tria, conditions improved. This young princess greatly encouraged
artistic revival which had made itself felt in Flanders at the beginning
1e 17th century.

RUBENS.—The Kermesse (detail). About 1635. Paris, Musée du Lou
The freeing of the instincts of a life always close to Nature is shown wit
restraint in the "Kermesses" which Rubens painted at the end of his lif

It was at this juncture that Rubens appeared upon the artistic st
He incorporated, so to speak, all the forces of Flemish art. By his
uralism and love of generous coloring, he is the direct descendant of
national Flemish School. During eight years in Italy, he devoted hin
especially to the study of the Venetians, the masters of color. Thank
the Italian Renaissance, he learnt what he could not find in Flanders:
art of composing large and dignified decorative paintings. Having retu
to Antwerp, Rubens settled there definitely and was named painter to
Archdukes. From then onwards he was to know only honors. He pai
more than 2,000 pictures, but often with the aid of collaborators, underta
all styles with the same audacity and sureness of execution. Rut
great superiority over his predecessors consisted in modeling directly
color. His forms are never inert or fixed, for his drawing is that of m

*sensuality of the magnificent nudes, with their full-blooded, pearly flesh
, is emphasized by the orchestration of red, green and gold. The composition is based on a sort of moving vortex.*

t, just as his colors are those of the passing reflection.   Nor should it be
otten that Rubens was a Fleming, with a decided penchant for opulent

ANTHONY VAN DYCK.—St. Martin Sharing his Cloak. About 1630.
Brabant, Church of Saventhem,

In this work of his youth, still conceived under the direct influence of Rub
Van Dyck differs nevertheless from his master by a certain aristocratic
languid grace.

RUBENS.—The Flight from Sodom (detail).   About 1625.   Paris,
Musée du Louvre.

richness of the reds stands out upon the silvery tones of the satiny fabrics
ch gleam under the fulgurating clouds.   The procession unrolls across the
composition like a garland.

and robust forms. His genius was characterized by movement, stren and healthy exuberance.

Rubens excelled in all styles: in religious scenes, in mythological subje in popular scenes and in portraits. Indeed he outlines the direction of for the two succeeding centuries. His followers in France were to be W teau and Delacroix, and through Delacroix, Renoir. The greatest Eng portraitists of the 18th century, Van Dyck and Reynolds, were also his dir descendants.

Rubens was one of the greatest figures of the Renaissance, eager to le and curious to understand all things. Admired, adulated, rich, happy, even enjoyed the favor of princes, while Philip II of Spain entrusted h with important missions. He was sent to London to negotiate the pe between Spain and England in 1630. Yet he desired to remain above things a painter.

Rubens had many collaborators and disciples. The most illustrious these was Van Dyck. On leaving his master's studio, Van Dyck trave in Italy and became a great portraitist thanks to studying Titian. He li for some time in Genoa, where he painted many portraits.

Jacob Jordaens, who enjoyed the friendship and advice of Rubens with being one of his pupils, was essentially Flemish, never having left Antw even to visit Italy. He was a builder of solid forms; his lighting was dir and rather crude, and his color somewhat earthy. Naturalism, expres in such somber accents by the Italians and Spaniards, becomes, under brush of the Fleming, an exuberant ode to joy.

David Teniers, heir to the tradition of Brueghel the Elder, depic humble Flemish life. He took pleasure in painting country scenes kermesses with a wholesome if rather crude boisterousness. His interp tation of these subjects is often witty; and though Louis XIV expressed greatest contempt for what he termed "Teniers' maggots," Don Juan Austria, brother of Philip IV, was one of his pupils.

The Flemings had long since discovered pure landscape. They realized that the representation of nature alone, separated from man, co be a work of art. At the end of the 16th and the beginning of the 17th c tury, the Bril brothers, who specialized in this subject, reduced it to cert laws, and thus were the first to define the principles of classical landsca They blended Italian poetic grandeur and simplicity, such as were expres by Giorgione and Titian, with the precision, sincerity and love of sm detail of the primitive Flemings. The 16th century tradition was ma tained in Rubens' day by a whole group of landscape, animal, still-life a flower painters. The most important of these is Jan Brueghel, also ca Brueghel de Velours (or Velvet Brueghel), the grandson of Brueghel the El

Other artists, who sometimes collaborated with Rubens, specialized

VELVET BRUEGHEL and HENDRIK DE CLERCK.—The Four Elements. Madrid, Museum of the Prado.

es which they treated in a decorative manner: Fyt and Snyders in still-
Paulus de Vos in animals, Van Uden in landscape, Cornelis de Vos in
traits, Gerard Seghers in flowers. The Flemish School continued to
.rish during the whole of the 17th century, then suddenly collapsed. At
end of the century, its decadence was everywhere apparent.

JORDAENS.—The King Drinks (detail).   Brussels, Royal Museum of Fine A
The joviality of Jordaens finds its source in a popular verve which is expre
without any restraint in manners or style.

SNYDERS.—The Parrots. Grenoble, Museum.

his animals, living or dead, Snyders has found a pretext for magnificent decorative effects.

DAVID TENIERS THE YOUNGER. — The Alchemist. Brunswick, Museum

Teniers is allied to the tradition which stems from Brueghel the Elder, tradit
known as "genre painting" and which is not concerned with important subjec
but rather draws its motifs from everyday life.

THONY VAN DYCK.—Charles I, King of England.   Paris, Musée du Louvre.

th the Louis XIV by Rigaud (p. 247), this portrait is the most handsome
·ness of a "Monarch," conceived, in true 17th century fashion, as the supreme
·ression of the superman.   Less solemn than Louis XIV, Charles I, with
his aristocratic ease, is really the "First Gentleman of the Kingdom."

REMBRANDT.—The Night Watch. 1642 Amsterdam, Rijksmuseum

THE DUTCH SCHOOL
OF THE 16th AND 17th CENTURIES

BEFORE any definite political division occurred between the Northern and Southern Provinces of the Low Countries, there were few artists who could be considered essentially Dutch. In the 15th and 16th centuries there was no difference between the painters of Haarlem and those of Bruges. But when Holland obtained her independence after a terrific struggle, her art was transformed, and great masters began to make their appearance. The United Provinces were maintained outside the influence of the Renaissance by their religion, race and history. Indeed, without

REMBRANDT.—Portrait of Saskia. Cassel, Gallery.

years of Rembrandt's marriage with Saskia Van Uylenburgh correspond
is "fashionable" and successful period. He likes to represent his young
wife attired in sumptuous robes, like some legendary princess.

Reformation, with its political, social and religious consequences, the Du
School might have continued to represent only an offshoot of the Flem
Once the Reformation came, painters no longer had to submit to the c
ates of King, Court or Church. Henceforth, they had only to please the
Republican bourgeoisie. This explains perhaps why they were interes
in depicting scenes of daily life, or in painting large "collective" pictu
in which were grouped the portraits of chief magistrates, aldermen or citi
of a town. They were less concerned with picturesque effects than v
expressing truth.

First among these Dutch artists was Frans Hals, who was essentiall
portraitist. He rendered the physiognomies of his models with infi
precision, naturalness, wit and good humor. Hals was a builder of s
forms rather than a painter of atmosphere. He endowed all things he ch
to depict with utmost the vivacity and spirit. His hands are the best ar
ulated and the most active in the history of art. An extraordinary inten
of life marks all his works.

Frans Hals gave lively expression to a style which had been practise
Holland for fifty years: collective portraits representing confraterni
boards, medical lecture halls. The figures stiffly rendered in earlier pict
by Dirck Barendsz, C. Keitel, Mierevelt, were depicted by Frans Hal
animated mood associated with the action that united them or associa
in the convivial gaiety of a banquet.

Frans Hals founded in Holland the tradition of "genre painting," re
senting the actions of everyday life. At first inspired by the rov
scenes of soldiery and common folk as depicted, for example, by Adri
Brouwer, Adriaen van Ostade, Jan Steen, genre painting about i
borrowed its themes from the ways of society. Gerard Ter Borch brou
about the transition between the two periods; although his pictures wer
small size, he was a great portrait painter.

Of all the minor masters of Holland, the exquisite Vermeer of Del
perhaps the most typically Dutch by virtue of the vast placidity and
fect serenity which form, so to speak, the background of his pictures. H
the painter of light and intimacy, of Dutch comfort and cleanliness. I
Van Eyck, he neglected no detail: a reflection glinting on a copper pot,
design of a carpet or the pattern of a dress were to him as important as
features of his personages, whose very soul he contrived to express.
was the painter of the tranquil, sheltered, somewhat secluded life of
women of his day.

Pieter de Hooch was the painter of Dutch interiors. He interpre
with great charm the serene, peaceful life of the bourgeois of Delft, in t
comfortable, well-cared-for homes, in which a ray of golden light slips thro
a window or an open doorway, glints on a fine copper pan or on hig

REMBRANDT.—The Syndics of the Cloth Hall (detail). 1662.
Amsterdam, Rijksmuseum.

ᵇared to the portraits of the Anatomical Lecture *of 1632 (p. 210), the*
ⁱcs of the Cloth Hall, painted in 1662, shows the progress of the expression
ner feeling in Rembrandt's work. The first canvas contains physical
portraits, the second calls forth spiritual qualities.

ʰed furniture. His subjects never appear hurried; their gestures are
ᵉrate. They take time to enjoy their calm, harmonious lives and to
ⁿplish their daily routine.
ᵒlland produced in the 17th century a great number of painters each of
ⁿ specialized in a particular style. Considering painting as a vast

REMBRANDT.—The Anatomical Lecture of Professor Tulp (detail).
The Hague, Mauritshuis.

FRANS HALS.—Portrait of a Young Man.   Berlin, Kaiser Friedrich Museum.

The joviality of Frans Hals is expressed in this smiling portrait which, with a gesture of welcome, seems about to leave the canvas to come towards the observer.

investigation into reality, they divided the task between them, sometim
assisting one another. Among the portrait painters (Thomas de Keyser, V
spronck, Morelse, N. Elias), some happily treated group portraits (Van
Helst, Van Ravesteyn). The portrait which was originally natural beca
mundane at the end of the century. Still-life painters excelled in express
"the silent life" of objects or foodstuffs set together on a table (Heda, Da
and Jan Davidz de Heem, W. Kalff). Genre painters were legion. Gera
Dou symbolized Dutch genre in a somewhat unfavorable manner, with pai
ing so precise as to be icy and lifeless. Among the animal painters, Cu
expressed the placidity of cattle, while Paul Potter depicted the anima
brute strength. The Dutch landscape painters reproduced all the aspects
Holland, the moist atmosphere of its canals (Van Goyen, Solomon
Ruysdael), its well-aligned towns (Van der Heyden, Berckheyden),
churches (E. de Witte), its skies towering above the earth (Jacob
Ruisdael, Hobbema), its grey sea and the ships that were making
fortune of the country (Van der Capelle, Vlieger, Van de Velde). Oth
were interested in the atmosphere of Italy (Van Berckem, Karel Dujard

It is therefore almost a surprise to note the appearance at this juncture
Jacob Van Ruisdael, who reminds one of a modern romanticist, for he
especially attracted by the more violent aspects of nature as sources
lyricism. Ruisdael is one of the masters who taught the 19th cent
the grandeur of melancholy. His works possess both majesty and st
he manifests a predilection for cloud-ridden skies, mournful sites
wind-racked trees. He is said to have visited Norway, Switzerland
Germany.

One name, however, towers above all others: that of Rembrandt,
glory of Dutch art. He was above all a portrait painter, like most of
artists of his race, but he was a portrait painter of the soul. His m
celebrated work, *The Night Watch*, is a group of portraits in action.
possessed, to the highest degree, imagination and a gift for invention wh
placed him and his school apart in Dutch art.

His mother had taught him to read the Bible, and his imagination of
strayed to the holy stories when not obsessed by reality. The art
Rembrandt oscillates between Amsterdam and the Land of Canaan; and
found the models for his Gospel and Biblical scenes in the famous Ghe
of the Dutch city.

Light is the very soul of his painting; it is by light and its contrast v
shadow that he expressed the drama of humanity and the love of God,
ecstasy of an apparition, the mystery of the soul, the truth of a face.
obtained the most striking effects by the way in which he either mingle
contrasted light and shadow. No one has acquired to a higher degree
science of contrast in composition.

REMBRANDT.—Christ and his Disciples at Emmaus.   1648.   Paris,
Musée du Louvre.

*nuances of light and shadow, Rembrandt expresses inner feelings.   Here,
light seems to shine from the face of Christ and fill the humble inn with a
supernatural presence.*

As a draughtsman, Rembrandt's technical skill was unrivaled.   Certain
awings, in their tranquility, show an intense gift of observation, Others,

PIETER CLAESZ.—Still-Life.   The Hague, Mauritshuis.

By their passion for still-life, the Dutch painters not only affirmed their gif[
observation and their taste for all the objects which concern everyday life, [
in a somewhat veiled manner, they also satisfied their purely artistic inclinati[
by attaining a skilful balancing of forms, and compositions secretly orde[
by geometric principles.

scrawled and vigorous, express the force of his creative imagination.
carries into his etchings his knowledge of the effects of light and shad[
and his genius of graphic invention.

After Rembrandt, the decadence of Dutch art was rapid.   It soon l[
its personal characteristics.   Holland fell under French influence and la[
mythological compositions replaced the familiar scenes or fine portraits
which Dutch painters had excelled.

FRANS HALS.—The Bohemian Girl. Paris, Musée du Louvre.

*rans Hals voluntarily leaves all the movements of his brush visible; he uses
a means of expression the very technique which the painters of the preceding
e covered up carefully under a smooth finish. The "brio" of his treatment
translates the gaiety of his temperament.*

Ter Borch.—The Singing Lesson. Paris, Musée du Louvre.

*A painter of inner feelings, Ter Borch takes pleasure in making his cold a
silvery tones sparkle softly in the half-light of his interiors muffled in silen
Even his concerts are rarely noisy.*

VERMEER.—Servant Girl with a Pitcher.   Amsterdam, Rijksmuseum.

light which bathes the humble servant girl in her familiar pose causes
to beam with a certain spiritual quality.   The objects themselves appear to
awaken to a higher form of life under the action of the magic radiance.

VERMEER.—The Girl with the Wine Glass.   Brunswick Museum.

This work from the early period of Vermeer's career still reflects a cer
accent of mundanity and affectation which are vestiges of the early stage
Dutch art.   Later, most often in solitary figures, Vermeer expresses noth
more than the serious silence of an inner dialogue.

PIETER DE HOOCH.—Young Woman in a Vestibule.   Amsterdam, Rijksmuseum.

ter de Hooch portrayed with kind affection the Dutch abode, sparkling h cleanliness under the effect of the sun which streams in through the large windows and which penetrates the entire house.

SOLOMON VAN RUYSDAEL.—Dutch Landscape.   Budapest Museum.

The uncle of Jacob Van Ruisdael, Solomon Van Ruysdael most freque
painted the river life of Holland with a picturesque and familiar acc

JACOB VAN RUISDAEL.—The Mill of Wijk-Bij-Oursteede. Amsterdam,
Rijksmuseum.

Jacob Van Ruisdael landscape is primarily a sky, often having its counter-
t on earth in a clear expanse of water—painting of the elements whose
ving force and immanence impose upon man a feeling of his smallness.

Velazquez.—Venus and Cupid: "The Rokeby Venus." London, Natic
Gallery.

This elegant picture is, before Goya, the only figure of a nude woman t
found in Spanish painting where religious prejudice prohibited a type of su b
cherished by the Italians.

ART IN SPAIN
IN THE 16th AND 17th CENTURIES

THERE existed several schools in Spain: those of Valencia, Tole
Madrid and Andalusia, but they were all dominated by the Schoo
Seville, whose most representative artist at the end of the 16th cent
was Juan de Ruela, the master of Francisco Herrera and of Zurba:
The latter painted some important compositions at Seville, but he
especially well-known for his monastic scenes and his solitary mc
praying in ecstasy.

Zurbaran, Herrera the Elder and Ribera were the Spanish painters who
t represented Catholic art. They were vigorous portraitists, faithfully
ying nature, with which they never took the slightest liberty. Their art
ays gives one the impression of seeking to surpass reality by intensity
expression. They are the painters of miracles and martyrs. Even the
ts of Herrera the Elder, whose often brutal paintings reflected his own
lent temper, reveal the same tormented features.

he founder of the modern Spanish school was in the 16th century the
tan Domenico Theotocopuli, better known as El Greco, who studied
some time in Venice with Titian, and came from Candia. His first
tures bear traces of their Venetian origin, as well as of the influence of
reggio and Michelangelo, though he remembered the Byzantine mosaics
is Near-Eastern birthplace. However, the works of El Greco executed
taly differ so slightly from those of the Venetian masters of the 16th
tury that in the absence of documents establishing his authorship, one
itates before attributing them.

n 1577, once in Toledo which "suited his nature" and where he knew
would obtain many orders, El Greco painted for the sacristy of the
hedral several pictures in which the Venetian influence is apparent. It
while painting the *Martyrdom of Saint Maurice* that he discovered his
mission which, as Maurice Barrès has said, "was to express in a realistic
nner the spasms of the life of the soul." At that time he abandoned his
m, golden coloring to adopt the tones used by the sculptors of poly-
ome statues. He even suppressed their blues, retaining only the yellow
re, reddish-brown tints, and especially the two fundamental colors of
old Byzantines—black and white. At the same time, El Greco began
elongate and twist his figures, with supreme contempt for the most
nentary rules of anatomy. He declared that he did this "in order to
ke them celestial bodies, just as we see lights which, considered from
r appear large to us, small though they may be."

lis activity was boundless: he painted, produced sculpture, built and
te. He is perhaps the author of the carvings of the great retable in the
rch of Afuera and of a group in polychrome wood showing the Virgin
ring the miraculous chasuble to Saint Ildefonso, which is now at the
inary of Toledo.

n the 17th century, various regional tendencies represented by painters
h as Ribera at Valencia, Herrera the Elder at Seville and Zurbaran were
jected to Italian influence. Ribera in his youth had lived at Naples.
had frequented the masters of Naturalism and in particular Caravaggio.
vision of reality which these artists expressed—whether sacred or
ane—were always coupled with a feeling of the latent picturesque and
matic elements in all scenes of life.

EL GRECO.—Holy Family with Bowl of Fruit. Cleveland Museum of A

One sees in this painting how the art of El Greco developed in contact with
Venetian School, and particularly with Tintoretto and the Bassanos; but
addition, by the modification of the coloring, the elongation of the proportio
and the twisting of the bodies, El Greco expresses the torment of the s

LUIS DE MORALES.—The Virgin Supporting the Dead Christ.   Madrid,
Academy of San Fernando.

*de Morales preceded El Greco in the expression of religious mannerism and
ent; but his style is different, as is well shown by a comparison with the
re on the opposite page: his art goes back to Flanders rather than to Italy.*

RIBERA.—The Club-foot (detail). Paris, Musée du Louvre.

Moved by the Christian sentiment of human weakness, the painters of S
often chose as subjects for their pictures beggars, idiots, or cripples.
art thus springs from a certain popular spirit instituted by Caravagg
whom Ribera was one of the most zealous supporters in Naples

ibera carried the contrast of light
shade to maximum intensity, in
manner of Caravaggio, drawing
n it magnificent effects of horror and
ism. Murillo was to remind all these
ent realists that there existed radiant
stial visions which they deliberately
ned to ignore. Murillo was a painter
isions. He had certainly studied the
positions of Raphael, as well as of
Flemish. But this did not prevent
from remaining realistic, like most
he artists of his time. He excelled
n art which expressed, in easily com-
ensible language, the tenderness,
asy and adoration of a naïve and
ound faith.

urbaran, the depicter of monks,
the most fervent religious painter
Spain, whose mystical passion he
oughly expressed. His art, found-
n violent contrasts of chiaroscuro,
more than any other, indebted to
avaggio.

ZURBARAN.—A Monk in Prayer.
London, National Gallery.

elazquez began by being the painter
odegones, i.e., still-life, kitchen tables and pictures representing popular
es. He owed much to Herrera, and his youthful works show the influence
urbaran. From 1624 to his death, he never left court except to undertake
official journeys to Italy. Living in the dreary Escorial Palace, he had
models the king, the royal family, the courtesans, jesters and even the
ses and dogs of the palace. He saw beyond appearances, and, in spite
heir sumptuous attire, he depicted the very souls of his subjects. It
nteresting to note that Velazquez greatly admired El Greco and even
sessed some of his works. He also studied with care the masterpieces
he Venetians which adorned the walls of the Royal Palace.

t was on the advice of Rubens that Velazquez traveled to Italy, where at
ice he was transported with enthusiasm before the works of Titian, Vero-
e and Tintoretto. On his return, his art was greatly modified. Hence-
h, atmosphere played a leading role in helping him shape living matter.
elazquez did not have an immediate following. Yet after Goya and
et, the naturalistic and Impressionist schools of the 19th century
claimed Diego Velazquez to have been a unique interpreter of life.

EL GRECO.—The Burial of Count Orgaz (detail).   Toledo, Church of S[
Tomé.—*It was by this masterpiece that El Greco compelled recognition in To[
He recounts a miracle: the apparition of St. Stephen and St. Alphonse con[
to give burial to the pious Count Orgaz whom one sees being received [
Heaven.   The figures become more unrealistic as they mount towards Hea[*

EL GRECO.—View of Toledo. New York, Metropolitan Museum of Art.

Greco painted various views of Toledo in several of his compositions; this the only one which comprises the entire canvas. Here Toledo appears like a fantastic, phantom city lighted by rays of the Apocalypse.

VELAZQUEZ.—Philip IV (detail).   Madrid, Museum of the Prado.

Velazquez imposes here the almost disquieting presence and the contracted a
worried countenance of the monarch who saw the decadence of the Spanish empi

[230]

GRECO.—Cardinal Nino de Guévara (detail).   New York, Metropolitan
Museum of Art.

*Greco goes so far in elongating the oval form of the Venetian faces that he
 ?s them an almond-shaped outline.   They are faces which seem to rise out
 of another world.*

ZURBARAN.—The Apparition of St. Peter the Apostle to St. Peter Nolasq
Madrid.

*A painter of Seville, Zurbaran worked especially in convents, with an aust
and truly monastic spirit. His simple, rigorous art ignores the outside wor
his figures move in an abstract environment, most often against a mysteriou
gloomy background : their power of apparition is all the more striking si
they are themselves painted in a most realistic manner, according to the tra
tion of Caravaggio. Here, Zurbaran has placed face to face the real p
sonage and the apparition—one almost as real as the other—without a
intermediary or accessory.*

ZURBARAN.—The Tears of St. Peter (detail). 1625. Seville, Cathedral, Altar of St. Peter.

s figure belongs to the Altar-piece of the Cathedral of Seville, one of the
t great works of Zurbaran. The 17th century's meditations on the problems
f the conscience gave a certain timeliness to St. Peter and his repentance.

VELAZQUEZ.—Portrait of the Infanta Margarita Teresa.   Vienna,
Kunsthistorisches Museum.

*The extraordinary robes of the Infanta are a wonderful pretext which per.
the magician of painting to put to work all the resources of his palette*

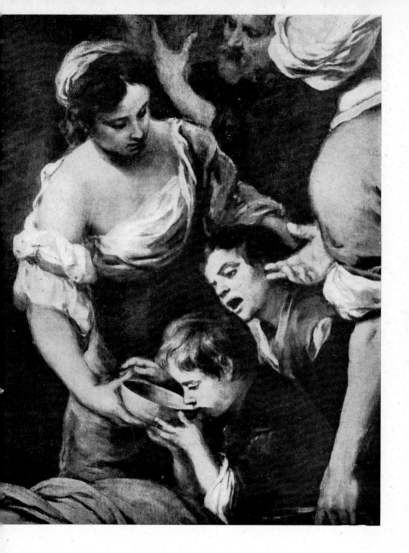

MURILLO.—Moses Drawing Water from the Rock (detail).   Seville,
Hospital de la Caridad.

*lamatory, superficial, and brilliant, Murillo's art well expresses the popular
piety of the Sevillians, lovers of processions and spectacles.*

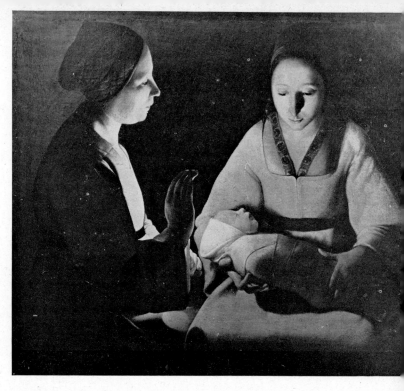

GEORGES DE LA TOUR.—The New-born Infant.   Rennes, Museum.

*A disciple of Caravaggism, Georges de La Tour represents the Nativity of C.
under the humble aspect of a rustic maternity, but with a high spiritual qua*

ART IN FRANCE IN THE 17th CENTURY

A T the beginning of the 17th century, the French school was not cle
defined.   True, Martin Fréminet, painter to King Henri IV, decor:
the Chapel of the Palace of Fontainebleau with vast compositions distin
reminiscent of Michelangelo.   He was followed by Simon Vouet, the
painter of Louis XIII, who was exceedingly precocious.   At the age of fourt
he already enjoyed such reputation as a portraitist that he was invite
England "to paint the portrait of a lady of quality."   He later followed
French Embassy to Constantinople where he enjoyed wide popula:

ILIPPE DE CHAMPAIGNE.—Portrait of a Man.   G. Wildenstein Collection.

llowing the tradition initiated by the Clouets, the French portrait during the
gn of Louis XIII is a psychological portrait, which seeks to express
lividual characteristics.   It is thus that Philippe de Champaigne, the
traitist of Port-Royal, has painted the austere face of this pious man, pre-
occupied with the grave problems of the conscience.

Vouet then visited Venice, Rome and Genoa, where he decorated the Do
Palace. He possessed a facile but superficial talent as a decorator.
did not prevent him from influencing most of the painters who were
illustrate the reign of Louis XIV, such as Le Brun and Mignard.

After the tumult of the Renaissance and the horrors of the religious w
a few artists in whom the study of old masters had not stifled all origina
began working for the court.

Philippe de Champaigne, who was born in Brussels but who early set
in France, brought from his native Flanders a robust naturalism, w
borrowing from the French School a taste for things of the spirit. He
came the favorite painter of Queen Marie de Medici and also of Richel
Being a friend of the celebrated Jansenist community of Port Royal,
shared their austere spirituality. His talent was honest and dignified,
his character, and his works are notable for their moral expression. H
weaker in his religious compositions, which are somewhat cold.

Le Sueur, one of Vouet's pupils, was less skilful but more amiable t
his master. His talent was more supple though less robust than tha
Philippe de Champaigne. He attracts by a certain *naïveté* of manner.

In Lorraine, Georges de La Tour, inclined to Caravaggism, a pai
whom the history of art has but recently discovered, carried on the asc
spirit of the Middle Ages. He was the painter of nocturnal light effects
represented sacred persons in the guise of common people, but transfigu
them by endowing them with expressions of sainthood and asceticism.

It was in the work of Nicholas Poussin that the national genius of Fra
realized itself once again. The destiny of this great artist is strange inde
although he conquered society in Paris, he could only create in Rome, s
rounded by the works of antiquity and the Italian 16th century mast
Raphael and Titian. He painted bacchanalia and lurid combats with
exuberance of youth. But French reason soon reasserted its rights a
disciplined him. Poussin now turned to severe, cold, historical compositic
which attracted the attention of Louis XIII and Richelieu. After so
difficulty, they persuaded Poussin to come back to France. He was, he
ever, unable to adapt himself to court intrigue and he soon returned
Rome, which he never left again. Poussin was, above all, a thinker,
works always dominated by reason. For him, painting was "the men
thing" that Leonardo da Vinci spoke of.

In his last years, Poussin chiefly cultivated landscape painting ; he g
its most perfect expression to classical scenes which makes nature the no
background of some heroic deed drawn from the Bible or mythology. M
French artists lived in Rome. The most celebrated among these, toget
with Poussin, was Claude Gelée, otherwise Claude Lorrain, who also sp
the greater part of his life in Rome. This artist's original gift of invent

POUSSIN.—Tancred and Erminia.   Paris, Musée du Louvre.

In this picture, Poussin takes his inspiration from one of the "romans courtois" (chivalrous novels) which were in vogue during the first half of the 17th century. His source is Tasso's "Jerusalem Delivered," which opposes the sublime and fatal loves of the crusader Tancred and the Saracen princess Erminia.

was, however, bounded by the limits of a classical ideal, expressed so
in landscape. In spite of his surroundings, Gelée's works remained m
French than Italian. His light, however, blends that of southern clir
—warm, golden, rich in powerful effects, but with a slight mistiness remi
cent of his native Lorraine. He had studied light under all its most var
aspects, from the first beams of dawn to the splendors of the setting s
Like Poussin, he loved to wander about the Roman countryside, captur
light in admirable wash-drawings. For more than two centuries, his w
exerted a strong influence on all artists who strove to depict the beauties
nature. He was greatly admired, particularly in England.

The Le Nain brothers, Antoine, Louis and Matthieu, have left picture
familiar scenes and of peasant life which throw an interesting light on
existence of humble French folk of their time. These pictures remind
of certain Dutch or Flemish masters, but the inspiration of the Le Na
dipped into the past of the French race and the silent, meditative dign
of their personages is in contrast with the unbridled instincts which
Dutch and the Flemings express when painting a similar subject.

During the reign of Louis XIV, French artistic activity was almost who
devoted to the service of the King. Indeed it could be said that dur
this period, French art was nationalized. In the first half of the reign, fr
1664 to 1690, not only were a few favorite artists retained almost forci
at court—as Velazquez was by Philip IV and Van Dyck by Charles I—
the whole of the French School which Colbert grouped together under
direction of Le Brun was called upon to work for the royal glorifi
tion. The state also undertook to train the artists and to organize th
work.

Le Brun, who visited Rome from 1642 to 1646, was introduced by Pous
to the masterpieces of antiquity. Endowed with great facility thou
little sensibility, he organized on returning to France an Academy of Pai
ing of which he was the first director. Appointed First Painter to
King, Le Brun undertook the decoration of the famous *Galerie des Glaces*
Versailles, where he retraced the glorious history of Louis XIV.

By his rare gift of imagination and the variety of his knowledge on
subjects, Le Brun was able to execute the "great intentions" of the ki
inventing what could best satisfy the whims of His Majesty. Secure
royal favor, Le Brun, who had a prodigious activity and facility for wo
reigned for twenty years over the destinies of French art. Alone Migna
who had lived for twenty-two years in Italy, might have disputed his supre
acy. Indeed, at the death of Le Brun, Mignard succeeded him as Fi
Painter to the King at the respectable age of eighty. Although Mignar
talent was superficial and facile, his skill in execution and the rath
studied grace of his figures won him favor. In 1663, he was asked

PHILIPPE DE CHAMPAIGNE.—Portrait of Cardinal Richelieu. Paris,
Musée du Louvre.

*is painting, where he emphasizes the sumptuous designs of the Cardinal's
Philippe de Champaigne still remembers the education he received in the
atelier of Rubens.*

PHILIPPE DE CHAMPAIGNE.—Portrait of Mother Catherine Agnès Arn
and Sister Catherine de Sainte-Suzanne.   Paris, Musée du Louvre

This work was painted by the artist as a votive offering for the miraculous cu
of his niece, the Sister Catherine de Sainte-Suzanne.   Here, she is recli
on a chaise longue and praying beside the Mother Superior of the co
of Port-Royal.   It is like an expression of the silence of the soul b
the Lord.

decorate the cupola of the Val-de-Grâce; Mignard also painted a numbe
portraits.

Several painters evolved a new style of portrait which was less intere
in the individual features of the sitter than his social status.   Largil
became the amiable painter of court beauties whom he disguised as
thological deities.   Rigaud has preserved for us the features of his g

LOUIS LE NAIN.—The Peasants' Meal. Paris, Musée du Louvre.

The French humanist spirit is expressed in these paintings where the Le Nain brothers have portrayed their peasants with an almost religious gravity which contrasts with the popular revelries of the Flemish and Dutch.

LE BRUN.—Portrait of Chancellor Séguier.   Paris, Musée du Louvre

A work of the youth of the artist who was to become the First Painte
Louis XIV, this painting still retains the noble simplicity of the tim
Louis XIII while already showing the pomp of the following reign.

temporaries : artists, writers, financiers, prelates, hereditary nobles and
se upon whom nobility had been conferred; he always represents them in
attering and dignified pose complying with the model given by the king
ₛself in the portrait he had commissioned Rigaud to paint. He composed
canvases with meticulous care, requiring assistance from his pupils and
ᵥing particular attention to the draperies, costumes and accessories of the
ting.

CLAUDE LORRAIN.—Antica Ostia. Madrid, Museum of the Prado.

Claude Lorrain is less engrossed in thought than Poussin. His art is rev
and he calls forth scenes of departure for far off regions where noble pal
are reflected in the clear water, golden-tinted by the setting sun.

HACINTHE RIGAUD.—Portrait of Louis XIV.   Paris, Musée du Louvre.

In this painting, Rigaud has given the perfect symbol of the "Ruler by Divine Right," as conceived by the 17th century.   The King is attired in his coronation ornaments; at his side he has the sword of Chilpéric which is still preserved today at the Musée du Louvre.

FRENCH ART IN THE 18th CENTURY

FRENCH art of the 18th century is at first distinguished by a lively reac
against that of the 17th. Life, fancifulness and spirit replaced
correctness and gravity which had characterized the preceding cent
Watteau was the most original master of the new school. He owed m
to the study of the Venetians and of the Flemings, especially to Rub
Having become the celebrated painter of his time, Watteau sought
describe, while idealizing them, the futile pleasures of the society in wl
he lived, and was received at the Academy under the title of Painter of
Fêtes galantes. His pictures, which have the enchantment of dreams,
full of grace and a discreet voluptuousness, but are often tinged wit
subtle melancholy. Watteau was also a witty observer, a fine draug
man and a warm and delicate colorist. He transposed the artificial lif
the *Régence* into tender and sentimental scenes of a delightful fantas

In spite of the shortness of his life, Watteau's output was considera
He possessed, more than any of his contemporaries, the feeling for nat
his graceful, rather whimsical figures generally disporting themselves
sylvan surroundings bathed in air and light.

Watteau left two pupils, Lancret and Pater, the latter, like his mas
born at Valenciennes. They carried the style of the *Fêtes galantes*
the reign of Louis XV. However Lancret often modified it with a touch
naturalism.

During the Regency and the reign of Louis XV, several painters create
new style, that of hunting pictures. They painted these scenes as a pret
for beautiful forest landscapes and the depiction of wild animals, horse
hounds from the royal packs. In this style they painted fine still-l
with game, silver plate and fruit.

During the reign of Louis XV, painting became more and more superfic
having as its main object panel decoration. Pictures represent mytholog
idylls centering around Venus, or else pastoral scenes. The influence of
theatre or the opera was very great. François Boucher is the most typ
of these decorative painters. A prolific worker, he produced pictures
Madame de Pompadour who, during the reign of Louis XV, ruled over
artistic life of the court.

It was Chardin, however, who saved painting of the period from be
taxed with frivolity. Drawing his inspiration from the Dutch (who enjo
a great vogue in the 18th century), he represented with touching simplic
the home life of the Parisian lower bourgeoisie. In his still-lifes he succeec
in expressing the poetry of everyday things by means of a splendid technic
which makes the observer feel the peculiar quality of each material.

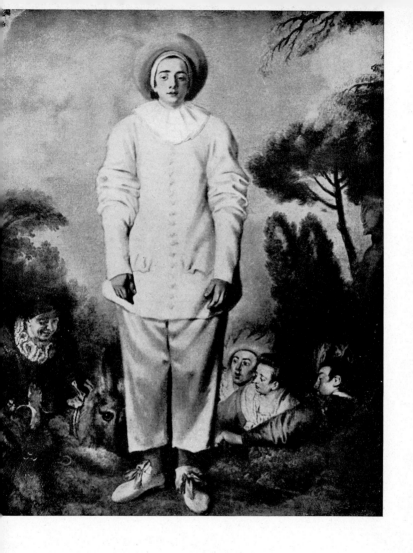

WATTEAU.—Gilles.   Paris, Musée du Louvre.

enes from the Italian theatre often inspired Watteau.   Here he presents the
wn, that ingenuous fellow with a warm heart whom Chaplin has to some
extent reincarnated on the screen.

BOUCHER.—Venus Consoling Cupid.   Washington, D. C., National Galle
of Art.

Boucher, who likes the harmonies of cold tones, excels in enclosing nudit
precious mother-of-pearl in a velvet case of royal blue.   The graceful movem
of the body is an expression of the curved forms of rococo style.

PATER.—The Bathers. Angers Museum.

*student of Watteau, Pater envelops his figures in a vaporous atmosphere
which gives his compositions the tonality of a revery.*

It was at this time the fashion for members of Parisian society to visit
e Salons in the hope of recognizing themselves in the pictures exhibited.
d, indeed, the leading personalities of the aristocracy live for us in these
rtraits. The pastels of Maurice Quentin de La Tour inimitably render the
pressions of vivacity, mobility and wit worn by subjects of Louis le Bien-
mé. La Tour is a true portraitist in the sense that any model, whether
ndsome or ugly, interested him and gave him the opportunity of seeking to
press a personality. He was a remarkable draughtsman who, with a few
m touches of gouache, could underline the dominant traits of a physiog-
my.
One of Boucher's pupils, the charming and delightful Fragonard, now

FRANÇOIS DESPORTES.—His Portrait as a Hunter, in a Landscape.   Pa
Musée du Louvre.

A painter of the King's chase, Desportes has represented himself surroun
by his dogs. This happy hunter is an expression of the smiling optimi
which the society of the 18th century enjoyed.   The movement of the body a
head is characteristic of Baroque composition, which is always in action.

peared upon the French artistic horizon. Like Watteau, he was the inter of love, but he lacked the latter's depth of feeling. For six months was an apprentice in Chardin's studio, then became a pupil of Boucher. e followed his master's counsel and studied Tiepolo in Italy. On his turn to France, he received many orders for decorative panels, having eady specialized in *gallant* subjects. After his marriage, however, Fragonard appears to have settled down and abandoned his libertine tendencies. His subjects became less amorous; he painted engaging scenes of mily life.

Greuze, curiously enough, was Diderot's favorite artist and one whom is trenchant critic persistently praised. Greuze revealed himself in the lon of 1755, presenting a new aspect of the taste of the day. His pictures ere wildly acclaimed, as the 18th century had just discovered that it was shionable to have feelings. His demure and simpering maidens, as pretty possible, lack naturalness, and all his compositions smack of artificiality. rtunately he was better as a portraitist.

The end of the 18th century weathered one of the greatest political up-avals of modern times. At first, these events did not have a noticeable fluence on painting, as the form of art which was eventually to characrize this period had actually evolved before the Revolution.

But a new trend was soon discernible. The first indication of the return the antique could already be noticed in the speech on Watteau which the unt de Caylus, an old friend of his, delivered at the Academy in 1748. everal years later, in 1755, the discoveries at Pompeii and Herculaneum oused interest in literary and artistic circles, even before the first blications of Winckelmann, the famous German archaeologist. In paint-g, Vien reacted against Boucher and the frivolous art of his school by intensive study of modeling and of antiquity. It was in Vien's studio at Jacques Louis David (who, curiously enough, had been a pupil of oucher before turning to Vien) learned the art of painting. He rejoined his aster who had been named Director of the French Academy in the Eternal ty. David studied antiquity, of which he sought to revive the traditions. Vith this in view, he painted *The Oath of the Horatii* which was exhibited in aris at the Salon of 1783 and created a considerable emotion. It was mposed according to all the rules of the new taste, which marked a return to istorical painting and the influence of Graeco-Roman antiquity.

After Robespierre's death, David was arrested, but he was soon released. ater, he supported the Empire and became first painter to Napoleon, who rdered from him several large decorative compositions.

The deep moral transformation which art underwent through David's fluence at this period resulted apparently from the importance given to the ought behind the work. Ever since Poussin, French art had tended to

WATTEAU.—The Sign of Gersaint. 1720. Right section (detail).
Berlin Museum.

This painting had been ordered by a friend of Watteau, Gersaint, who had a
antique shop on the Pont-au-Change and who wished to use the painting as
sign for his store.   It was exposed only fifteen days, as it shortly found a buye
It was purchased in 1756 by Frederick II of Prussia.

WATTEAU— The Embarkation for Cythera (detail). 1717. Paris, Musée du Louvre.

his picture was painted by the artist as his canvas for his reception to the
cademy of Painting and Sculpture. It is a sort of pantomime which unrolls in
procession of amorous couples whose attitudes express all the nuances of desire.

NICOLAS DE LARGILLIÈRE.—Portrait of the Painter, his Wife, and Daught
(detail).   Paris, Musée du Louvre.

The brilliant and fluid coloring of this picture indicates the influence
Rubens' art which was then still new in the French School and which the criti
of the time opposed to the art of Poussin.   The young girl who is singing h
taken on the "inspired" air of the opera singers of the period.

LANCRET.—The Dance in the Pavilion (detail). Potsdam, Palace.

is painting shows a happy gathering in a large circular salon which opens
a park. Lancret, lost in his dreams even more than Watteau, chose as his
jects the amusements of the refined and carefree society of the 18th century.

JEAN-MARC NATTIER.—Portrait of a Young Woman (detail). Paris,
Musée du Louvre.

Jean-Marc Nattier had made a specialty of pompous portraits showing subje
particularly women, disguised as the divinities of Olympus. After 17
however, he rejected all that pomp in favor of a genuine simplicity.

BOUCHER.—Diana Resting after her Bath, with one of her Companions.
Paris, Musée du Louvre.

these crystalline nudes which shine with a soft radiance amidst the reeds,
age and symbols of the hunt, Boucher prolongs an ancient French tradition,
that of the nymphs of the School of Fontainebleau.

rifice the expressive element to purely decorative preoccupations. Le
.n, and especially the 18th century artists, had produced pictures to
use and please; it was David who restored its dignity to thought. As
ortraitist, he remains one of the greatest names of the French School.

FRAGONARD.—Monsieur de La Bretèche, brother of the Abbé de Saint-No
Private Collection.

All the jauntiness of the century, all of Fragonard's gay and impulsive sp
burst forth in the laughter of this figure portrayed with all the vigor of
artist's frenzied brush.

MAURICE QUENTIN DE LA TOUR.—Mademoiselle de Chastagne de Lagrange.
Saint-Quentin Museum.

Maurice Quentin de La Tour is a psychologist who analyzes deeply the soul of his models. His pastel technique, which goes back to drawing more than painting, serves his analytical tendency. One sees here the development of Clouet's portrait-drawings.

CHARDIN.—The Marketer. 1739. Paris, Musée du Louvre.

Chardin painted the daily life of the Parisian lower middle-class with a p̶
found sympathy ; his unctuous technique of painting with a full brush is deri
from the Le Nains and the Dutch masters.

Élisabeth-Louise Vigée-Lebrun.—Portrait of Madame Vigée-Lebrun
and her Daughter (detail).   Paris, Musée du Louvre.

*The influence of Neo-Classicism is perceptible in these regular figures modeled
in the ancient manner, and in the smooth, uniform technique which imitates
the polished surface of statues.*

CHARDIN.—The Bun. Paris, Musée du Louvre.

Slowly modeling his objects in rich layers of paint, Chardin imparts to th
the warmth of a sort of spiritual life which they derive from their humble ▪
as human auxiliaries.

FRAGONARD.—The Bathers. Paris, Musée du Louvre.—*This is the most
stunning of all the paintings of Fragonard: a splashing of flesh-like tones,
reds and greens, where the artist recaptures that magic fluidity which
animates all the elements of Rubens' canvas with a Dionysian sensuality.*

WATTEAU.—Jupiter and Antiope. Paris, Musée du Louvre.—*In this painting Watteau reveals one of his sources : the art of Titian, which he was able to examine at great length in the works preserved in the*

ENGLISH ART
IN THE 17th
AND 18th CENTURIES

ᴀᴄ Oliver.—Lucy Harigton, Countess
Bedford. London, Victoria and Albert
Museum.

ENGLAND appears late in the cycle of modern art. Her insularity had kept her apart from the diverse artistic influences of the Continent. During the Romanesque period, monastic activity was particularly brilliant in Ireland, which was far from the invasions and violence of other lands. Gothic architecture also assumed a magnificent, almost unrivaled development on the northern side of the Channel, but the plastic arts were singularly behindhand.

One notes, however, in the 16th and 17th centuries, the names of certain artists, such as that of Nicholas Hilliard, painter to Queen Elizabeth, who brought to his large portraits the rather dry, minute qualities of his remarkable talent as miniaturist. There was also Isaac Oliver, Hilliard's pupil, whose miniatures were celebrated, and George Jamesone, who studied in the atelier of Rubens at Antwerp, where he met Van Dyck. Jamesone has left some good portraits in which the influence of the two great masters is distinctly noticeable. There existed nevertheless in England a monarchy and a cultivated aristocratic society which welcomed foreign artists, giving them important orders, and lavishing on them honors and titles of nobility. Thus it was that, attracted by the generosity of their English patrons, the most celebrated portraitists of Europe settled at the court of England. One after the other, Holbein, Antonis Mor, Rubens, Van Dyck became, so to speak, English painters, over a longish period of their lives. The last-named in particular, Anthony Van Dyck, married the daughter of a nobleman and died in London. By virtue of the supreme elegance of his portraits, he can be called the father of the English school of painting. Van Dyck trained a few English pupils, Dobson, Jamesone and the miniaturist Cooper. His real successors were, however, foreigners like himself. The Dutchman Van der Faes (1618 to 1680), who was to become Sir Peter Lely, continued to depict the aristocracy.

ANONYMOUS MASTER.—Portrait of Queen Elizabeth.   London,
National Gallery.

The existing portraits of Queen Elizabeth, for the most part anonymou
preserve the memory of the extraordinary robes, bedizened with embroidery a
jewels, which the imperious and stylish sovereign liked to wear.

n the meantime, Rubens had made large decorations for James I, but
the end of the 17th century the French masters in turn crossed the
nnel to seek their fortune in England. Their influence lasted until
middle of the next century, by which time national art had established
lf. Hogarth and Reynolds, who were the first typically English
resentatives, appeared a whole century after Rubens, Rembrandt,
azquez and Poussin.

Villiam Hogarth, who was the son of a printer's overseer, was the first
ly English painter. Witty and satirical like Swift and Sterne, his pitiless
s of observation and satire—often ribald—express themselves in a famous
es of paintings in which the vices and depravity of the times were casti-
ed. Hogarth used to say that he "painted Comedy," and that he con-
ered it "a work of public utility." For Hogarth, painting was at times a
torial sermon or lesson in morals, at others a biting, vengeful satire such
ve encounter later in Goya or Daumier. His tragedies always end by the
imph of virtue. In the portraits he has left, Hogarth reveals himself
reat painter. His satire was not solely directed towards the defects of
aristocracy. He denounced pitilessly the grossness of the lower classes
l painted a series of pictures in which he protested against the cruelty of
n towards animals, for which he had a passionate attachment. He never
red to strike hard as long as he hit the mark, and it is certain that his
uence on the society of his time was considerable. He preferred to con-
er himself as "an author, rather than as an artist," and as such, his place
y the side of the great satirists Thackeray, Fielding, Cervantes, Molière.
The English school has a marked personality, essentially insular and,
ving been born after the Renaissance, it remained a stranger to the world
mythology, history and Christian legend which had nourished the
aginations of other nations. Like the Dutch school of the 17th century,
is naturalistic and began by being almost exclusively devoted to
trait painting before turning its attention to landscape.

Hogarth can be said to have been the founder of the English school of
rtraitists. It was he who influenced the most cultured, refined, intelli-
t and cosmopolitan of English artists, the first President of the Royal
ademy, Sir Joshua Reynolds. No greater contrast could be imagined than
se two men and their works. Although never a pupil of Hogarth,
ynolds certainly owed more to him than to his official master, Thomas
dson. Having spent three years in Italy, Reynolds' debt to the great mas-
s of the past, Titian, Raphael and Michelangelo, as well as to the Bolognese,
immense. He studied them as a craftsman and student of aesthetics, in
ler to assimilate that part of their genius which might allow him to give
country a worthy art. In one of his celebrated speeches at the Royal
ademy, Reynolds declared: "In order to recover the Grand Style, that

dead language which one might call the Language of the Gods, one sho
have continually before one's eyes the works of Michelangelo, the pla
casts of his statues, the copies of his drawings, the engravings of
paintings."

In Reynolds' large studio in Leicester Square, where he gathered
admirable works of art acquired during his travels, the most celebra
society beauties and actresses of England came to pose. In each of
portraits, Reynolds attempted new effects. He was particularly succes
in his delightful likenesses of children.

Thomas Gainsborough equals him in fame and, today, is often prefer
to him. Who were Gainsborough's first masters during his earliest stay
London between 1741 and 1745? His biographers are rather undecided ab
this. No doubt he studied in the atelier of Francis Hayman, a hard-drink
friend of Hogarth. But Hayman's advice does not seem to have left a
trace in Gainsborough's work. Such is not the case with his French mas
Gravelot, and one cannot deny that the spirit of Watteau, transmitted
Gravelot, is noticeable in Gainsborough's admirable crayon preparations
his portraits of women. Like Reynolds, Gainsborough was a great color
and his works were more sensitive and perhaps more delicately grace
than those of his great contemporary. Van Dyck was his master and mo

Gainsborough is also the creator of the great school of English landsc
painters. He often complained of being obliged to remain a portr
painter since his landscapes found little favor.

Reynolds and Gainsborough dominate the whole school of English p
trait painting from the inaccessible height of their genius. But a
degrees lower down, two other artists excel in this kind of painting: Romn
and Raeburn. Romney began as a carpenter in his father's workshop,
at seventeen entered the studio of a certain Christopher Steele, whom he so
left, abandoning even his wife and two children to go to London; he also w
to Italy. Romney's first pictures had a great success. His vogue
portraitist became extraordinary, thanks to his rapidity of execution a
his skill in modifying the ravages of time and nature in the features of
beautiful models. Like all the English portraitists of the 18th centu
Romney had the faculty for portraying women. In common with his t
celebrated rivals, he had as models the most famous personages of his tir

Sir Henry Raeburn was the national painter of Scotland, and ma
members of the great clans posed for him. His talent was characterized
a great sincerity of craftsmanship, by richness of coloring and a great resp
for the individual truth of his models.

Hoppner, who imitated Reynolds, has left several impassioned portra
of *Lady Hamilton*. His pictures of young people are full of charm and ra
merit, although his talent was superficial and facile.

GAINSBOROUGH.—Mrs. Charles Tudway (detail).   Paris, Knoedler
Collection.

*d is the favorite color of the English; it has long been in wide use both for
litary uniforms and for judicial robes. The English painters have used
it easily to create brilliant effects.*

PETER LELY.—Young Girl with a Parrot.   London, Tate Gallery, Millbank

Peter Lely succeeded Van Dyck as painter to the court; he was himself
Flemish origin.   Like   his   master,   he   is   adept   at   giving   his   model
aristocratic appearance and a mannered elegance.

R William Dobson.—Endymion Porter.   London, National Gallery.

e talent of William Dobson, a student of Van Dyck, evokes the frank, natu-
istic art of the Flemings. Endymion Porter, despite his martial air, was a
ron and lover of the arts, as the presence of the bust of Seneca indicates.

WILLIAM HOGARTH.—Marriage à la Mode. Scene II. Shortly after Marria
London, Tate Gallery, Millbank.

The puritan spirit of a certain part of English society is manifest in this se
of satirical paintings on the mores of the time which were suggested to Hoge
by the novel and the theatre.

WILLIAM HOGARTH.—Hogarth's Servants.　London, National Gallery.
hen he is not preoccupied with moralizing, Hogarth abandons himself to pure joy of painting familiar models with a full and skilful brush.

RICHARD WILSON.—Landscape. Paris, Musée du Louvre.

Richard Wilson, who spent six years in Italy, brought back to England
Italian style of landscape, covered with golden mists, which he borrowed fr
Claude Lorrain, whose works had henceforth a great success in England

GAINSBOROUGH.—The Blue Boy. U. S. A., Huntington Collection.

uinsborough resided at the spa of Bath, where English society sought refined version during the Georgian period. To him are due the most aristocratic figures of English painting.

SIR JOSHUA REYNOLDS.—Nelly O'Brien. 1760. London, Wallace Collectio

This is the portrait of a "femme de joie," quite fashionable in the society of the
time of George III. She exhales a sort of carnal wholesomeness which o
does not find again until much later in Renoir's feminine portraits.

GAINSBOROUGH.—Miss Elizabeth Singleton.   London, National Gallery.

*mpared to Nelly O'Brien, Miss Singleton appears quite marked by romantic
lancholy.   This difference in character comes less perhaps from the models
n from their painters.   Gainsborough seems to have found the source of this
dreamy melancholy in the art of Watteau.*

GEORGE STUBBS.—The Gentleman Holding a Horse.   London, Tate Galle:
Millbank.

It was England, where equine sports have always been in great favor, th
created the type of painting having for object the exaltation of the beauty
horses.   Stubbs made an entire series of portraits of celebrated race hors

FRANCIS HAYMAN.—Three People in a Landscape. London,
Mrs. Derch Fitzgerald Collection.

*...yman, who was the master of Gainsborough, is an admirable painter of
...bject pictures. Where his pupil would have created a poem, he amuses
with an anecdote.*

JOHN HOPPNER.—Portrait of a Young Woman and Boy.   Paris,
Musée du Louvre.

This picture clearly shows the turning point of English painting, which pass
at the end of the 18th century, from a Rubens-like vigor to the polished craf
manship of Neo-Classic and antique influence.

SIR HENRY RAEBURN.—Portrait of Captain Robert Hay of Spot. Paris,
Musée du Louvre.

*The best works of Raeburn, the painter of Scottish society, are his military
portraits in which he is adept at expressing a soldierly bearing; magnificent
uniforms he delighted in painting with a full brush.*

SIR JOSHUA REYNOLDS.—John and Theresa Parker. Saltram,
Collection of the Count of Morley.

Painting's most charming figures of children are due to the English artis
In accordance with his lively temperament, Reynolds sees in them the symb
of youthful grace and wholesomeness.

GAINSBOROUGH.—The Painter's Daughters.   London, National Gallery.

*Gainsborough, more of a poet than Reynolds, paints spiritual rather than phys-
al traits; he is moved by the fragile charm of childhood, and casts on these
youthful countenances a premature shadow of melancholy.*

FRANCIS WHEATLY.—The Rat Trap. Paris, Knœdler Collection.

*In addition to its great portraitists, at the end of the 18th century the Engl
School included many minor masters who painted subject pictures inspired
the Dutch School, but in a more neo-classic style.*

GOYA.—La Maja Desnuda.   Madrid, Museum of the Prado.

SPANISH PAINTING IN THE 18th CENTURY

8TH century Spanish art presents a very unequal aspect.   Whether we consider Luis Melendez, Bayeu, Mariano Salvador Marcella or José Castillo, we see only second-rate artists.   Assuredly, there is no lack of interest in their portraits and frescoes and in the scenes from popular life which they have left us, but had Goya not illuminated Spanish painting by his brilliant and varied talent, art in the Iberian peninsula during the 18th century would have no history.

Goya, who appeared in the second half of the century, is in a way the heir of Velazquez.   Thanks to Goya, after almost a century and a half of decadence, Spanish painting was renewed.   Though less perfect, he was definitely more varied than his great master.   He ignored nothing of the art of painting, and was equally original as a draughtsman, lithographer and etcher.   Unlike Velazquez, he only attained mastery in his art by dint of hard, unremitting work.   Goya had already passed his fortieth year before he produced the works on which his reputation now rests.   By the combination of lyricism and comedy, pathos and satire, Goya reminds one of Cervantes.   Like El Greco and Velazquez, he is a great portraitist.   Indeed this type of painting is the foundation of his art, and even, in his pictures of pure imagination, one recognizes the peculiar vision of a portraitist.   This

EL S.ᵒ D.ᵉ CARLOS IIII REI DE ESPAÑA, Y EMPERADOR DE LAS YNDIAS. GEFE Y SOBERANO DE LA REAL Y DISTINGUIDA ORDEN ESPAÑOLA DE CARLOS III SU AUGUSTO PADRE, Y COMO GRAN MAESTRE DE ELLA, MANDO VARIAR EL MANTO DE LOS CABALLEROS EN LOS TERMINOS QUE DEMUESTRA ESTE RETRATO, PROTECTOR BENEFICENTISSIMO DE ESTA REAL ACADEMIA DE S.ᵗ CARLOS DE NUEVA ESPAÑA, QUE FELIZMENTE REYNA. AÑO DE 1792.

MARIANO MAELLA.—Charles IV.   Mexico City Museum.

While Goya innovated a painting of romantic expression, Mariano Mael
influenced by the German Rafael Mengs, who had settled in Madrid, practis
an academic style.

Luis Melendez.—Still-Life. Paris, Musée du Louvre.

also true of the masterpieces of El Greco and Velazquez. The *Burial of Count Orgaz*, *Las Meninas* and Goya's *Family of Charles IV* may be classed in the same category of plastic creation.

Goya may be said to have renewed and innovated every form of art he challenged. He was always unexpected; there was nothing conventional about him. His cartoons for tapestries prove that he had studied Boucher and Fragonard. He is the author of the finest nude in Spanish painting: *La Maja Desnuda*; but he also had his hours of Christian inspiration, as when he painted the *Last Communion of Saint Joseph*. This is one of the finest religious paintings of the 18th century; in infinite gradations of twilight grey, it pulsates with mystery. Goya is truly the father of modern art.

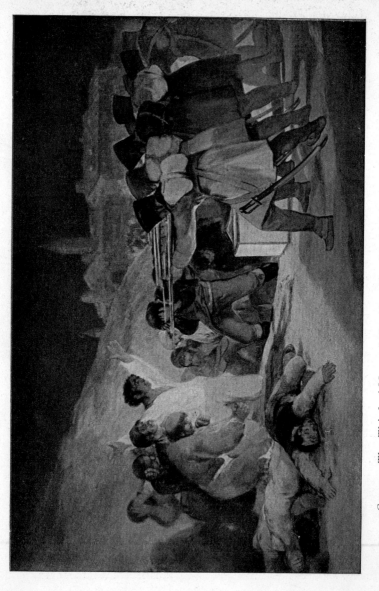

GOYA.—The Third of May, 1808 (detail). Madrid, Museum of the Prado.
Painted in 1814, at the time of the Restoration, this picture, which is the pendant of the "Second of May,"

GOYA.—Dona Gumersinda Goicœcheay. About 1808. Paris,
Collection of the Vicomtesse de Noailles.

*ccording to the Velazquez tradition, Goya often silhouettes his portraits
gainst an abstract background which lends to the subject a somewhat phantom-
like appearance.*

GOYA.—King Charles III in Hunting Attire. 1786. Madrid,
Duque de Fernan Nuñez Collection.

Goya seems to have taken pleasure in painting with cruelty the weaknesses a
the physical and moral defects of the last Bourbons of Spain. One wonde
how these paintings could have pleased their princely patrons.

ROBERT FEKE.—The Family of Isaac Royall. Harvard Law School,
Harvard University, Cambridge, Mass.

*ainted in 1724, this is perhaps the earliest "conversation piece" by an American
tist. Its realism in portraiture contrasts with a similar, earlier work of
Smibert upon which it was based.*

MERICAN ART IN THE 17th AND 18th CENTURIES

⌐HERE is a literary legend that Christopher Columbus brought an artist
with him to depict the India he believed to have reached. In actual
ct, art had no more place in the opening up of the North American coastline
an in a gold rush. Survival was the all-important question; the amenities
uld come later. Surprisingly, one artist did assist at the founding of the
oanoke Colony, a certain Joannes With (or John White), who, about 1685,
companied explorers to the back country as a reporter. But the early
lgrim landings were without the benefit of a chronicler. At that juncture
e "artificer" with brush and palette was a supernumerary on the rock-
und New England coast. Early meeting-houses were severely undecorated.

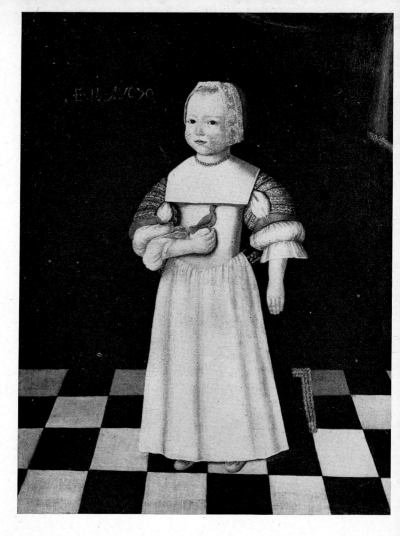

ANONYMOUS.—Portrait of Henry Gibbs, 1670. Collection of Mrs. Alexand
Quarrier Smith.

*Identified solely as the Freake Limner (after a family whose portraits he pair
ed), this journeyman painter shows the true primitive's inborn sense of desi*
and interest in detail.

BENJAMIN WEST.—Colonel Guy Johnson. Mellon Collection,
National Gallery of Art, Washington, D. C.

child prodigy who in 1759 departed for England there to indoctrinate succes-
e generations of young Americans with the foreign painting ideal, West
quently applies European conventions to sturdy American material, as here,
where he places a Redskin in front of the classic half-drawn curtain.

GUSTAVUS HESSELIUS.—Lapowinsa.
Historical Society of Pennsylvania
Collection.

Painted in 1735, this commissioned likeness of an Indian chief ranks among America's earliest outstanding objective documents. Its author, born in Sweden, was at his best when, as here, he follows a realist bent rather than imitating the popular graces of the day.

Life was a matter of wrestling living out of a stony land over short a season. Under these cumstances, it is a wonder th there actually exists an Americ portrait dated 1641, signed W. presumed to be one William Rea It needed a full generation befo the journeyman painter arrived type of artisan who traveled abo the land selling signs, coats-of-ar to the gentry and, when occasi demanded, filling in the face on stock portrait with a male, fema or juvenile likeness.

To the first Americans, the family portraits—these tangi ancestors—gave a sense of t permanence and security they h left behind. The early works sta ed a tradition, and as a result, t portrait remained the princip mode of art expression until t 19th century. Its first exponer provided the most picturesq phase of American art. Unskille tight and conventionalized, the "primitives" tell us a great ma fascinating things about peop and manners of the time. T typical journeyman painter w English. He ground his own colors and got commissions mostly in t summer time, when he could travel from town to town, receiving an where from $10 to $40 for a portrait. Two of the best exponents of th genre are the recorders of the Gibbs and Freake families. Designed wi natural grace, if not conventionally pretty, they exhibit that sense of rea ity which, even today, is a mainstay of American art.

The most important early signed work came from Continentals. T German Justus Engelhardt Kühn worked in the vicinity of the aristocrat colony of Baltimore and catered to the builders of the first fine house One of his best-known paintings shows a seven-year-old squire in form 18th century dress attended by a young Negro slave, carefully pose

JOHN SMIBERT.—Nathaniel Byfield. Metropolitan Museum of Art, New York.

This Scottish-born artist, educated in London, inspired by trips to Italy, brought European savoir-faire to his paintings of prominent citizens.

gainst a sham setting of architecture and formal garden. The Swede Hesselius, who worked in Delaware, also played up the European note in a

GILBERT STUART.—Mrs. Richard Yates. Mellon Collection, National Gallery of Art, Washington, D. C.

Perhaps the solidest piece of painting from the brush of the renowned por traitist of George Washington, this work embodies the best trait of America painting—that transcending honesty which can turn even a defect into a element of art.

similar canvas that depicts young Master Calvert. Hesselius' adult howerer, are often less idealized and show a glum long-facedness which typically early American. His portraits of Indian chiefs are fascinating an authentic documents.

In Nieuw Amsterdam and up the Hudson River valley, the Dutchma Pieter Vanderlyn painted the Dutch patrons in all their stately stiffnes

JOSEPH BLACKBURN.—The Winslow Family.   Museum of Fine Arts, Boston.

lowing in the "conversation piece" tradition of Smibert and Feke, Black-
n undertakes a group picture with confidence, combining the fashionable
ndon mannerisms of gesture or drapery with stock facial expressions and the
basic rigidity of the provincial.

moved from the influence of the English colonizers as it was from the
guenot settlers of the Carolinas, this Dutch school occasionally introduces
vivid note from the mother country, notable in background still-life or an
asional reference to Rembrandt's dramatic chiaroscuro.

With the arrival from Scotland of a forty-year-old painter called John
ibert, a purely British type of art took over, admired especially in Boston,
asioning in 1730 the first art exhibit ever recorded in America.   Smibert
ported the popular English conversation piece, or group picture of a prom-
nt family shown in its entirety at home.   His *Dean Berkeley and*
tourage, painted before 1730, shown three-quarters length, took social
ecedence over any mere head.   The idea soon spread.   Eleven years
er, the American-born Robert Feke painted the wealthiest citizen of
ston, Isaac Royall, complete with three female relatives, baby and Turkey

JOHN SINGLETON COPLEY.—Mr. and Mrs. Isaac Winslow.
Museum of Fine Arts, Boston, Mass.

Painter of New England's mercantile aristocracy, Copley's portraits are acc
plished, sympathetic and brilliantly analytical. This one dates from be
1774, when he departed for England, leaving behind him the American s
which is estimated as his finest period.

carpet. This latter picture is more naïve than the first, for Smibert h
not only worked in England, but made copies of old masters on the Contine
Yet in its very lack of fine gesture, it holds a peculiar charm fortified by
artist's natural feeling for light and color. Two other British-born pai
ers, John Wollaston and Joseph Blackburn familiarized the Colonies w
the styles of London's most popular painters, Sir Peter Lely and, lat
Sir Godfrey Kneller. Wollaston painted the prominent Tidewater fami
such as Randolphs and Carrolls, and the Custis children, this latter wo
described as "of a very pretty taste." Blackburn rendered New Englan

JOHN TRUMBULL.—George Washington. Metropolitan Museum of Art, New York. *As aide to General Washington during the Revolution, Trumbull was able to give an eye-witness account of historic scenes and also painted a first-hand likeness of the Father of his Country. Artistically, however, he remains something of a dilettante.*

THOMAS SULLY.—Queen Victoria.   Metropolitan Museum of Art, New Yo

An aimiable painter who carried into the 19th century the English traditions
the 18th, Sully is notable for his charming coloring and an engaging style e
when depicting an unprepossessing subject.

ng mercantile aristocracy, generally at three-
rter length, which allowed some play of drapery,
tain and column, certain elegant gestures of the
ds. To this period must be added the name of
emiah Theus, a Swiss artist, who embellished
rigid figures with bright color and a surface
sh that earned for him a highly successful career
South Carolina.

ohn Singleton Copley was born in Boston in 1737.
a child he received sound art instruction from his
p-father Peter Pelham, who was a dancing mas-
as well as a painter. He lived to render the
ebrities of his day in the fine clothes which the
rchants of New England could by now well
ord. Painted with understanding, scrupulous
e and natural skill, his work hits a happy
dium between the crude if veracious provincial
l the would-be exponents of the Grand Manner.
oley marks the turning-point between a subser-
nt Colonial art and a true native style. The
ses of his sitters are arresting in their uncon-
tionality. His *Boy with Squirrel*, shown at the
ndon Society of Artists in 1766, was the first
mple of American painting to earn laurels
road. A Tory by marriage, Copley fled to
gland just before the Revolution. He continued
paint there but with a difference, his early work
ng considered by far his finest.

CHARLES WILLSON
PEALE.—The Stair-
case Group. Museum
of Fine Arts, Phila-
delphia.

*In the tradition of the
forthright early Amer-
ican limners is this
rare picture dated
1795, by an artist
whose versatility often
threatened his genuine
painting talents.*

Copley went to London at the invitation of the
at 18th century expatriate, Benjamin West.
Quaker child prodigy, West at an early age
ne under the influence of William Williams, one
the most mysterious and fascinating figures in
whole history of American art. Williams,
ose autobiography of his experiences as a shipwrecked mariner
s later avidly read by Byron, painted conversation pieces combining
wealth of imaginative detail with theatrical, stilted charm. West soon
nt abroad, studied in Rome, settled in London (where he received
yal commissions and enjoyed the friendship of Sir Joshua Reynolds),
ere to open a school in which, for half a century, American painters
rned their ABCs. His was a long-term influence, ranging from Matthew
att, born in 1734, to Samuel F. B. Morse, who died in 1872. President

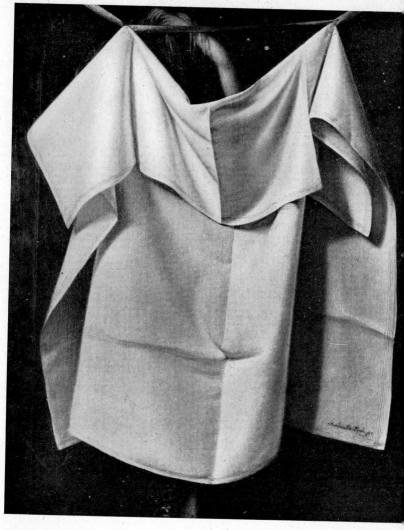

RAPHAELLE PEALE.—After the Bath. William Rockhill Nelson Galle
Kansas City, Mo.

*Forerunner of the Surrealists in the often enigmatical character of his wo
and his interest in purely objective effects, this artist is responsible for some
the earliest still-lifes in American painting.*

he Royal Academy in London for eighteen years, a kindly man who
riended, housed and boarded many a young American, West was a
unch believer in tried, classical forms. His one adventurous excursion
o semi-reality affected later documentary artists such as Trumbull. This
t "machine," called *The Death of General Wolfe*, contrary to usage,
victed the leader and his mourners in garb wihch approximates the actual
e of dress they wore instead of the classic toga.

Matthew Pratt, born in 1734, lived in West's London house for two years
l came home to become Philadelphia's first painter. Of his English visit
has left a charming record entitled *The American School*, which describes
st and his eager young apprentices in a lively discursive manner that
cedes 19th century genre. John Trumbull, once General Washington's
e, was bailed out by West when he was imprisoned in London as a
el. His *Battle of Bunker Hill* is reputed to be an eye-witness account.
s color is handsome, his grouping deft. Charles Willson Peale is one
the interesting characters of this epoch. A born tinkerer (he repaired
tches, made saddles, stuffed animals), he is reputed to have become
erested in painting following a visit to Copley in Boston. He, too,
led for London and the mecca of West's studio. Peale has the distinc-
n of having painted Washington in his prime (Gilbert Stuart recorded
old age) as a sturdy, spell-binding man of arms. He depicted the
volutionary leaders and, later, displayed their portraits above cases of
ffed animals in the celebrated museum which he founded in Philadelphia.
veral of his sons made names for themselves in subsequent American

Considerable controversy has raged as to the respective merits of Copley
d Gilbert Stuart. The former epitomizes the American view. The latter,
ough uninfluenced by his study with West (he was his assistant for four
urs), found immediate favor in London for his vaporous, sophisticated
le, eventually receiving as much as 30 guineas for a likeness. A
endthrift, Stuart's financial involvements led him to Ireland and, even-
ally, back to the country of his birth. Here he determined to paint the
at leader, George Washington. He created three portraits, known
ough association as the Vaughan, the Athenaeum and the Lansdowne
pes. Of these he made something over 100 replicas. As the latter are
signed, and in turn tempted artists as prominent as Sully to copy them,
ey remain a subject of much argument. Stuart worked with light,
most frothy colors, underpainting in white lead. In many of these
ashington pictures, the madders and vermilions have faded. However,
tight-lipped *Father of his Country* remains the accepted version, and at
best is unquestionably an extremely accomplished piece of painting. The
s-known side of Stuart is represented by his superb portrait of

Mrs. Yates in the National Gallery, as pertinent and observant as anyth in American art.

Charles Willson Peale named his children after the artists he admi Rembrandt, Titian, Raphaelle, Angelica Kauffman. Of the lot, Rapha seems the most significant today for his quality of pure painting and objec observation, which expressed itself in some of the first still-lifes painte America. Rembrandt Peale painted the principles of the War of 1812 the "Porthole" Washington. A late West pupil was Thomas Sully, depi of pretty, well-bred, pink-and-white women and children, in the taste of English 18th century. Already, however, he represents a throw-back earlier modes. With the inevitable time-lag, American painting was lowing in the footsteps of American politics. By the end of the 18th cent it was blazing a trail which, if not of rugged individualism, is at le honest and distinctive, commensurate with the spirit of the new lan which it was born.

BIBLIOGRAPHY

CHRISTIAN ART

LPERT. — Die Malereien der Katakomben Roms (2 volumes) ; 1904.

LPERT. — Die römischen Mosaiken und Malereien der kirchlichen Bauer vom IX. bis XIII. Jahrh.; Freiburg-in-Brisgau, 1916 (second edition, 1917).

N BERCHEM and E. CLOUZOT. — Mosaïques chrétiennes du IVe au Xe siècle ; Geneva, 1924.

BREHIER. — L'Art chrétien ; Paris, 1918 (second edition, 1928).

DIEHL. — L'Art chrétien primitif et l'art byzantin ; Paris, 1928.

BYZANTINE ART

M. DALTON. — Byzantine Art and Archæology; Oxford, 1911.

M. DALTON. — East Christian Art: A Survey of Monuments; Oxford, 1925.

WULFF. — Die Altchristliche Kunst von ihren Anfängen bis zur Mitte des ersten Jahrausend ; Berlin, 1918.

WULFF and M. ALPATOFF. — Denkmäler der Ikonenmaler ; Hallera, 1925.

BREHIER. — Art byzantin ; Paris, 1924.

. DIEHL. — Manuel d'art byzantin (second edition) ; Paris, 1925-1926.

MOURATOFF. — La Peinture byzantine ; Paris, 1928.

YFORD PIERCE and ROYALL TYLER. — L'Art byzantin (2 volumes) ; 1932.

ABAR. — Art byzantin ; Paris, 1938.

LEMERLE. — Le Style byzantin ; Paris, 1948.

CARLOVINGIAN ART

NITSCHEK and H. MENZEL. — Die Trier Ada Handschrift ; Leipzig, 1889.

BEISSEL. — Geschichte der Evangelienbücher in der ersten Hälfte des Mittelalters ; Freiburg, 1906.

KOHLER. — Die Karolingischen Miniaturen (2 volumes) ; Berlin, 1932-1934.

ÉDÉE BOINET. — La Miniature carolingienne ; Paris.

11th AND 12th CENTURIES

MALE. — Histoire de l'art (under the direction of André Michel) (II, 2) ; 1905.

CILLON. — Peintures romanes des églises de France ; Paris, 1938.

CH. OURSEL. — Les Miniatures du xiie siècle à l'Abbaye de Cîteaux ; Di
1926.

GOTHIC ART

H. MARTIN. — Les Miniaturistes français ; Paris, 1906.

H. MARTIN. — La Miniature française du xiiie au xve siècle ; Paris, 1923

G. VITZHUM. — Die Pariser Miniatur Malerei ; Leipzig, 1907.

A. HASELOFF. — Les Psautiers de saint Louis ; M. Soc. Art. Fr., 1899.

F. DE MELY. — Le Miniaturiste parisien Honoré ; R. A. A. M., 1910.

J. L. FISHER. — Das architektonische Problem der Glasmalerei ; 1914.

COMTE DURRIEU. — Les Très Riches Heures du Duc de Berry ; Paris.

ITALIAN ART IN THE 13th AND 14th CENTURIES

VENTURI. — Storia dell'Arte italiana (VII) (4 volumes) ; 1911-1915.

TOESCA. — Storia dell'Arte italiana (Il Mediœvo) ; 1927.

R. VAN MARLE. — The Development of the Italian Schools of Paint
(17 volumes) ; The Hague, 1923-1937.

L. HAUTECŒUR. — Les Primitifs Italiens ; Paris, 1931.

G. BAZIN. — Les Primitifs Italiens ; Paris.

J. ALAZARD. — L'Art italien des origines à la fin du xive siècle ; Paris, 19

LUIGI COLETTI. — I. Primitivi (I. dell'Arte benedittina a Giotto) (194
II. I Senesi e i Giotteschi (1946) ; III. I Padani (1947).

GARRISON. — Italian Romanesque Panel Painting ; 1949.

O. SIREN. — Toskanische Maler im XIII. Jahrh. ; Berlin, 1922.

OFFNER. — A Critical and Historical Corpus of Florentine Painting ; 19
1949.

E. CECCHI. — Trecentisti senesi ; 1928.

JOHN POPE HENESSY. — Sienese Quattrocento Painting ; London, 19

THE BEGINNING OF THE RENAISSANCE

A. SCHMARSOW. — Italianische Kunst im Zeitalter Dantes (2 volume
Augsburg, 1928.

VENTURI. — Storia (V) ; Rome, 1906.

VAN MARLE. — The Development of the Italian Schools of Painting (II to
The Hague, 1925.

BERENSON. — The Italian Painters of the Renaissance ; London, 1932.

BERENSON. — The Drawings of the Florentine Painters (3 volumes) ; 19

NTURI. — Le Origini della Pittura veneziana ; Venice, 1907.

STI. — Storia della Pittura veneziana ; 1910.

BAZIN. — Les Primitifs Italiens (2 volumes) ; Bergamo.

BAZIN. — Fra Angelico ; Paris, 1949.

ESCA. — Masolino ; Bergamo, 1908.

LMI. — Masaccio ; 1934.

LMI. — Paolo Uccello, Andrea da Castagno, Domenico Veneziano.

LONGHI. — Piero della Francesca ; 1927 (French translation, Officina ferrarese ; Rome, 1934).

DE. — Botticelli (Klassiker der Kunst) ; 1926.

P. HORNE. — Botticelli ; London, 1908.

NUTI. — Il Perugino (2 volumes) ; Siena, 1931.

OCCO. — Mantegna ; Bologna, 1927.

MBA. — Giovanni Bellini ; Paris, 1938.

MBA. — Viatico per cinque secoli di Pittura veneziana, Florence, 1946.

FLEMISH ART IN THE 14th AND 15th CENTURIES

RIEDLÄNDER. — Altniederländische Malerei (14 volumes) ; Berlin, 1924-1937.

RIEDLÄNDER. — Von Van Eyck bis Brueghel ; Berlin, 1921.

WINKLER. — Altniederländische Malerei ; Berlin, 1924.

ERENS GEVAERT. — Histoire de la peinture flamande des origines à la fin du xvᵉ siècle (3 volumes) ; Paris and Brussels, 1927-5930.

HULIN DE LOO. — Critical Catalogue of the Exhibition of Bruges ; 1903.

WINKLER. — Die flämische Buchmalerei des XV. und XVI. Jahrh. ; Leipzig, 1925.

OOGEWERFF. — De Nederländische Schilderkunst (5 volumes) ; The Hague, 1936-1947.

BEENKEN. — H. und J. Van Eyck ; Munich, 1941.

I. DE TOLNAY. — Le Maître de Flemalle et les frères Van Eyck ; Brussels, 1939.

SCHONE. — Thierry Bouts ; Berlin, 1938.

DESTREE. — Hugo van der Goes ; Basel, 1923.

I. DE TOLNAY. — Bosch ; Basel, 1937.

RMAIN BAZIN. — Memlinc ; 1938.

EO VAN PUYVELDE. — L'Agneau mystique ; 1949.

EO VAN PUYVELDE. — Les Primitifs Flamands ; Paris 1947.

GERMAN ART IN THE 14th AND 15th CENTURIES

E. HEIDRICH. — Altdeutsche Malerei (Die Kunst in Bildern) ; 1909.

F. BURGER, H. SCHMITZ, I. BETH. — Die deutsche Malerei vom a
gehenden Mittelalter bis zum Ende der Renaissance (3 volumes) ; Ber
1913-1924.

W. HAUSENSTEIN. — Tafelmalerei der deutschen Gothik ; Munich, 19

C. GLASER. — Die altdeutsche Malerei ; Munich, 1924.

C. GLASER. — Les Primitifs Allemands ; 1931.

A. STANGE. — Deutsche Malerei der Gothik (3 volumes) ; Berlin, 1934-19

W. R. DEUSCH. — Deutsche Malerei des fünfzehnten Jahrhundert ; 1936.

A. HULFTEGGER. — Évolution de la peinture en Allemagne et dans l'Eur
centrale ; Paris, 1949.

FORSTER. — Die Kölner Malerschule vom Meister Wilhelm bis Steph
Lochner ; Cologne, 1923.

BROCKMANN. — Die Spätzeit der Kölner Malerschule ; Bonn, 1924.

FRIEDLÄNDER. — M. Schongauer ; Leipzig, 1923.

ZÜLCH. — Der historishe Grünewald : Mathis Gothardt Neithardt ; Muni
1938.

FRENCH ART IN THE 15th CENTURY

J. MESNIL. — La Miniature française aux xve et xvie siècles ; Paris, Brusse
1930.

P. A. LEMOISNE. — La Peinture française à l'époque gothique, xiv^e
xve siècles ; Leipzig 1931.

LOUIS DIMIER. — (Series of articles : Gazette des Beaux-Arts : July, Aug
December 1936 ; November 1937 ; September, November 1938.)

JACQUES DUPONT. — Les Primitifs Français ; Paris, 1937.

G. BAZIN. — La Peinture française des origines au xvie siècle ; Paris, 1937.

L. REAU. — La Peinture française du xive au xve siècle ; Paris, 1939.

CH. STERLING. — Les Peintres du Moyen Age ; Paris, 1941.

GRETE RING. — A Century of French Painting; London, 1949.

GRETE RING. — La Peinture française du xve siècle ; Paris, 1950.

PAUL WESHER. — Fouquet und seine Zeit ; Basel, 1945 (French editio
1945).

CH. STERLING. — Chef-d'œuvre des Primitifs Français : Le Couronneme
de la Vierge, par E. Quarton ; Paris, 1938.

O. SMITAL and F. WINKLER. — Herzog René d'Anjou, Livre du Cœ
d'Amour épris ; Vienna, 1926.

SMITAL and F. WINKLER. — Le Cœur d'Amour épris ; Éditions Verne, 1949.

ABANDE. — Les Brea, peintres niçois des xve et xvie siècles en Provence et en Ligurie ; Nice, 1937.

SPANISH AND PORTUGUESE PAINTING
UNTIL THE END OF THE 15th CENTURY

C. POST. — History of Spanish Painting (II to V) ; 1934.

ATALONIAN FOUNDATION OF THE UNIVERSITY OF PARIS. — La Peinture catalane à la fin du Moyen Age ; 1932.

LAFUENTE FERRARI. — Breve Historia de la pintura española ; 1946.

ARQUES DE LOZOYA. — Historia del arte hispanico (III) ; 1940.

ORMO. — Rodrigo de Osona, padre e hijo y en escuela ; Archivo español de arte y arqueologia, 1932-1933.

ANCHEZ-CANTON. — Tablas de Fernando Gallego en Zamora y Saladogia ; 1929.

DE FIGUEREIDO. — O Pintor Nuno Gonçalves ; Lisbon, 1909.

EGENDRE aud HARRIS. — La Peinture espagnole ; Paris.

GUINARD et J. BATICLE. — La Peinture espagnole ; Paris 1950.

ITALIAN PAINTING IN THE 16th CENTURY

ENTURI. — Storia dell'Arte italiana (IX) (7 books) ; 1925-1934.

ERENSON. — The Italian Painters of the Renaissance ; Oxford, 1930.

. PITTALUGA. — La Pittura italiana del Cinquecento ; Florence, 1932.

ALLUCHINI. — La Pittura veneziana del Cinquecento (I and II) ; Novara, 1944.

ILDEBRANDT. — Leonard de Vinci ; 1927.

UIDA. — Leonard de Vinci und sein Kreiss ; Munich, 1929.

ODMER. — Vinci ; Stuttgart, 1931.
atalogue of the Da Vinci Exhibition at Milan ; 1940.

ELTRAMI. — Luini ; Milan, 1911.

USTI. — Michel-Ange ; Leipzig, 1900.

H. DE TOLNAY. — Michel-Ange (3 volumes) ; Princeton, 1940-1949.

ELBER. — Raphael (2 volumes) ; Stuttgart, 1933.

RONAU. — Raphael ; Stuttgart, 1904.

RICCI. — Correggio ; Rome, 1929.

ODMER. — Correggio e gli Emialiani ; Novara, 1943.

. FROHLICH-BUM. — Parmesan und der Manierismus ; Vienna, 1921.

QUINTAVALLE. — Il Parmigianino ; Milan, 1948.

SUIDA. — Titien ; Zurich, 1933 (French edition, 1935).

H. TIETZE. — Titien — Leben und Werk (2 volumes) ; Vienna, 1937.

G. BRIGANTI. — Il Manierismo ; 1947.

L. BECHERUCCI. — I Manieristi toscani ; Novara, 1944.

FRENCH PAINTING IN THE 16th CENTURY

DIMIER. — Histoire de la peinture française des origines jusqu'au retour
Vouet (1300-1627) ; 1925.

MOREAU-NELATON. — Les Clouet et leurs émules ; Paris, 1923.

GEBELIN. — Le Style Renaissance ; Paris, 1942.

P. DU COLOMBIER. — L'Art de la Renaissance en France ; Paris, 1945.

THE SCHOOL OF FONTAINEBLEAU

P. DAN. — Trésor des merveilles de Fontainebleau ; 1642.

LABORDE. — Renaissance des arts à la Cour de France (2 volumes) ; 185
1853.

LABORDE. — Comptes des bâtiments du Roi (1571) (2 volumes) ; 1879-188

HERBET. — Les Graveurs de l'École de Fontainebleau ; 1896-1902.
Catalogue of the Exhibition of the School of Fontainebleau ; 1939.

DIMIER. — Le Primatice ; Paris, 1900.

KUSENBERG. — Le Rosso ; 1931.

M. ROY. — Jean Cousin ; Sens, 1909.

LEBEL. — Caron (Amour de l'Art, 1937 and 1938 ; Bulletin de la Société
l'Histoire de l'Art français, 1949 ; Burlington Magazine, 1950).

GERMAN ART IN THE 16th CENTURY

F. BÜRGER. — Die deutsche Malerei von ausgehenden Mittelalter bis zu
Ende der Renaissance ; Berlin, 1921.

G. GLUCK. — Die Kunst der Renaissance in Deutschland ; Berlin, 1928.

W. R. DEUSCH. — Deutsche Malerei des XVI. Jahrh. ; Berlin, 1935.

WEINBERGER. — Nürnberger Malerei und die Anfänge der Dürerschule
Strassburg, 1921.

H. TIETZE and E. TIETZE-CONRAT. — Dürer kritisches Verzeichn
(2 volumes) ; Basel, Augsburg, 1937-1938.

FR. WINKLER. — Die Zeichnungen A. Dürer (3 volumes) ; Berlin, 193
1938.

ÖLFLIN. — Die Kunst A. Dürer ; Munich, 1943.

. DEUSCH. — Hans Holbein der Jünger ; Berlin, 1938.

RIEDLÄNDER. — Altdorfer ; Berlin, 1923.

VON BALDASS. — Altdorfer ; Vienna, 1941.

RIEDLÄNDER and J. ROSENBERG. — Die Gemälde von Lucas Cranach; Berlin, 1933.

POSSE. — Lucas Cranach ; Vienna, 1942.

. CURJEL. — Hans Baldung Grien ; Munich, 1924.

STUMM. — Nicolas Manuel Deutsch als bildender Kunstler ; Berne, 1925.

ANOFSKY. — Albrecht Dürer (2 volumes).

THE RENAISSANCE IN THE LOW COUNTRIES

AREL VAN MANDER. — Het schilder-boek ; Haarlem, 1604. (English translation: Van de Wall: Dutch and Flemish Painters; 1936.)

J. HOOGEWERFF. — Vlaamische Kunst en italianische Renaissance ; 1935.

RIEDLÄNDER. — Gossaert ; Berlin, 1930.

D. MICHEL. — Brueghel ; Paris, 1931.

H. DE TOLNAY. — Brueghel ; Brussels, 1935.

RIEDLÄNDER. — Altniederländische Malerei (volumes VI to XIV) ; Berlin, Amsterdam.

USTAVE GLÜCK. — Pieter Brueghel the Elder ; Paris 1938.

ITALIAN ART IN THE 17th AND 18th CENTURIES

OSS. — Die Malerei der Spätrenaissance in Rom und Florenz (2 volumes) ; Berlin, 1920.

OSS. — Die Malerei des Barok in Rom ; Berlin, 1925.

JETTI, DAMI, and TARCHIANI. — La Pittura italiana del Seicento e del Settecento ; Milan, 1924.

. NEBBIA. — Pittura italiana del Seicento alla mostra di Palazzo Pitti ; Novara, 1942.

. LONGHI. — Viatico per cinque secoli di Pittura veneziana ; 1946.

. G. LORENZETTI. — Pittura italiana del Settecento ; Novara, 1948.

. ROUCHES. — La Peinture bolognaise à la fin du XVIᵉ siècle ; Paris, 1913.

. DELLA PERGOLA. — I Carracci ; Bergamo, 1932.

ARANGONI. — Caravaggio ; Florence, 1922.

AHN. — Caravaggio ; Berlin, 1928.

ARLO. — Le Caravagisme ; Aix-en-Provence, 1941.

FLEMISH ART IN THE 17th CENTURY

FRIEDLÄENDER. — Die niederländischen Maler der XVII. Jahrh. ; Berl 1926.

R. OLDENBOURG. — Die flämische Malerei des XVII. Jahrh. ; Berlin, 192

W. VON BODE. — Die Meister des Holl. und Vlämischen Malerschul Leipzig, 1917.

E. MICHEL. — La Peinture flamande au XVIIe siècle ; Paris, Hypérion, 19.

FROMENTIN. — Maîtres d'autrefois.

J. BURCKHARDT. — Erinnerungen aus Rubens ; Vienna, 1938.

MAX ROOSES and CH. RUELENS. — Correspondance de Rube (6 volumes) ; Antwerp, 1897-1919 (New abridged edition in 2 volume P. Colin, 1927).

PROSPER ARENTS. — Geschriften van en over Rubens ; Antwerp, 1940.

MAX ROOSES. — L'Œuvre de P. P. Rubens, Histoire et description de s tableaux et de ses dessins (5 volumes) ; Antwerp, 1886-1892.

F. R. LEHMAN. — P. P. Rubens Menschen und Mächte des Barock ; Stut gart, 1936.

GLUCK. — Van Dyck (Klassiker der Kunst) ; Stuttgart and Berlin, 1931.

MAX ROOSES. — Jordaens, sa vie et ses œuvres.

DUTCH SCHOOL OF THE 17th CENTURY

CORN. HOFSTEDE DE GROOT. — Beschreibendes und kritisches Ve zeichnis der Werke der hervorragendsten holländischen Maler des XVI Jahrh. (20 volumes) ; Esslingen, 1907-1928.

FRIEDLÄNDER. — Die niederländischen Maler des XVII. Jahrh. ; Propylæ Berlin, 1923.

L. HOURTICQ. — Hollande (Arts Una) ; 1923.

G. BAZIN. — Les Grands Maîtres de la Hollande.

R. GROSSE. — Niderländische Malerei der XVII. Jahrh. ; Berlin, 1936.

KEPPEL. — Dutch Painters of the XVIIth Century and their times; T Hague, 1933.

WALTHER BERNT.—Die niederlandischen Maler der XVII. Jahrh.; Munic 1948.

W. VON BODE. — Frans Hals, sein Leben und seine Werke (2 volumes) Berlin, 1914.

A. BARTSCH. — Catalogue raisonné de toutes les estampes qui forme l'œuvre de Rembrandt, Vienna, 1897.

C. NEUMANN. — Rembrandt ; 1902 (third edition, 2 volumes, 1922).

ORN. HOFSTEDE DE GROOT. — Jan Vermeer von Delft und Carel
Fabritius ; 1906.

B. DE VRIES and R. HUYGHE. — Jan Vermeer de Delft ; Amsterdam, 1948.

. VON STECHOW. — Ruisdæl ; Berlin, 1938.

ART IN SPAIN IN THE 16th AND 17th CENTURIES

16th

ACHECO. — Arte de la pintura en antiguedad y grandeza ; Seville, 1649.
(Republication : 2 volumes ; Madrid, 1866).

. VON LOGA. — Die Malerei in Spanien von XIV. bis XVIII. Jahrh. ; Berlin, 1923.

GUINARD et J. BATICLE. — La Peinture espagnole ; Paris 1950.

EGENDRE and HARRIS. — Histoire de la peinture espagnole ; Paris,
1934.

. L. MAYER. — El Greco — Kritisches und illustriertes Verzeichnis des
Gesamtwerkes ; Munich, 1926.

EGENDRE et HARTMANN. — El Greco, œuvres complètes ; Paris 1936.

17th

USTI. — Velazquez und sein Jahrhundert (2 volumes) ; Bonn, 1888.

AYER. — Velazquez ; Berlin, 1923.

. KEHRER. — F. de Zurbaran ; Leipzig, 1918.

. MAYER. — Murillo (Klassiker der Kunst, second edition) ; Stuttgart,
1913.

FRENCH ART IN THE 17th CENTURY

. DIMIER. — Histoire de la peinture française du retour de Vouet à la mort
de Le Brun (1627-1690) ; I, 1926 ; II, 1927.

V. WEISBACH. — Französische Malerei des XVII. Jahrhundert ; Berlin,
1932.

ROUCHES. — Le Sueur ; Paris, 1923.

OUIN. — Charles Le Brun et les arts sous Louis XIV ; Paris, 1889.

H. STERLING. — Les Peintres de la réalité en France au XVIIe siècle (third
edition, 1934).

PARISET. — Georges de La Tour ; Paris, 1949.

SARLO. — Les Le Nain (Renaissance, p. 1 to 58) ; 1928.

AMOT. — Les Le Nain ; Paris, 1929.

). GRAUTOFF. — N. Poussin, sein Werk und sein Leben ; Munich, 1914.

RIEDLÄNDER. — Claude Lorrain ; Berlin, 1921.

FRENCH ART IN THE 18th CENTURY

LES GONCOURT. — L'Art au XVIIIe siècle ; 1859-1875, 1909-1910.

P. MARCEL. — La Peinture en France au début du XVIIIe siècle ; 1913.

L. HOURTICQ. — De Poussin à Watteau ; 1921.

L. REAU. — Histoire de la peinture française au XVIIIe siècle ; 1926.

L. GILLET. — La Peinture de Poussin à David ; 1935.

R. HUYGHE. — La Peinture française du XVIIIe et du XIXe siècle ; 1938.

L. HOURTICQ. — La Peinture française au XVIIIe siècle ; 1939.

L. DIMIER. — Les Peintres français du XVIIIe siècle ; 1928-1930.

L. DIMIER. — Les Maîtres du XVIIIe siècle ; 1943.

M. FLORISOONE. — La Peinture française : Le XVIIIe siècle ; 1948.

RATOUIS DE LIMAY. — Le Pastel en France au XVIIIe siècle ; 1946.

J. ROMAN. — Le Livre de raison de H. Rigaud ; 1919.

HILDEBRANDT. — Watteau ; Berlin, 1922.

HEROLD, VUAFLART and DACIER. — Jean de Julienne et les graveurs Watteau (4 volumes) ; 1923-1929.

M. J. PARKER. — The Drawings of A. Watteau; 1931.

INGERSOLL-SMOUSE. — Pater ; 1928.

WILDENSTEIN. — Chardin ; 1933.

BESNARD and WILDENSTEIN. — Catalogue de La Tour ; 1928.

P. MANTZ. — Boucher, Lemoine et Natoire ; 1880.

A. MICHEL. — Boucher ; 1908.

ENGLISH PAINTING IN THE 17th AND 18th CENTURIES

COLLINS BAKER and CONSTABLE. — English Painting of the XVI t century and of the XVII ; London, 1830.

JOHN ROTHENSTEIN. — An Introduction to English Painters; London 1933.

W. T. WHITLEY. — Artists and Their Friends in England (1700-179 (2 volumes) ; 1928.

S. COLOMB. — La Peinture anglaise ; Paris 1947.

KLINGENDES. — Hogarth and English Caricature; London, 1944.

W. R. ARMSTRONG. — Gainsborough ; 1899 (second edition, 1904. Frenc translation, 1904).

SPANISH PAINTING IN THE 18th CENTURY

ARQUES DE LOZOYA. — Historia del arte hispanico (volume IV); Barcelona, 1945.

. GUINARD et J. BATICLE. — La Peinture espagnole ; Paris, 1950.

ERUETE Y MORET. — Goya (3 volumes) ; Madrid, 1916-1918.

. L. MAYER. — Goya ; Madrid, 1923.

ANCHEZ-CANTON. — Goya ; 1929 (French translation).

ADHEMAR. — Goya ; Paris, 1941.

. ALBAREDA. — F. Bayeu y Subias ; Aragon, 1934.

AMERICAN PAINTING IN THE 17th AND 18th CENTURIES

GNES ELEANOR ADDISON. — Romanticism and the Gothic Revival ; New York, 1938.

AMUEL ISHAM. — History of American Painting ; New York, 1936.

AMES THOMAS FLEXNER. — First Flowers in Our Wilderness ; Boston, 1947.

OLGER CAHILL and ALFRED BARR, Jr. — Art in America ; New York, 1935.

OMER SAINT-GAUDENS. — Survey of American Painting ; Pittsburg, Carnegie Institute Department of Fine Art. — Catalogue to the Carnegie exhibition, 1940.

WALKER. — Great American Paintings from Smibert to Bellows ; New-York, 1944.

W. McSPADDEN. — Famous Painters in America ; New York, 1907.

. W. SHELDON. — American Painters with Examples of their Work ; London, 1879.

BIOGRAPHIES

A

CRTSEN, Pieter. Flemish School. About 1507/1508-1575. (Pages: 174, 175.)—Freemaster at Antwerp in 1535, he painted several altar pictures, but mainly still-lifes and market scenes which he treats with great breadth of style. He had as pupil his nephew Joaquim Beuckelaer (about 1533-1573), who painted the same themes.

LTDORFER, Albrecht. German School. About 1480-1538. (Pages 156, 157, 165.)—A painter and engraver of Regensburg, where he was probably born, Altdorfer's early works show a keen sense of landscape (*St. George*, 1510, Munich). With the exception of the large altar-pieces of St. Florian, he mainly painted panels of small dimensions. In 1529 he executed his masterpiece, *The Battle of Alexander* (Munich), for William of Bavaria. He had a great number of disciples and imitators.

NGELICO. GUIDO DI PIETRO, in religion FRA GIOVANNI DA FIESOLE, called IL BEATO. Italian School. Florence, 1587-1455. (Pages: 33, 34, 36, 39.)—At the age of twenty he entered the Dominican monastery at Fiesole. He was undoubtedly formed by Dom Lorenzo Monaco and underwent the influence of the School of Marches, especially of Gentile da Fabriano. After the gracefulness of his early works, there followed an attempt at spatial expression (1433, *The Coronation of the Virgin*, Louvre, Paris). Between 1439 and 1445 he decorated the cubicles and certain rooms of St. Mark's Monastery at Florence where the Dominicans of Fiesole had established themselves. Called to Rome in 1445, he painted there certain frescoes which have now disappeared. In 1447, at the San Brizio Chapel of the Dome at Orvieto, he began the decoration which Signorelli was to finish. In the frescoes of the studio of Nicholas V at the Vatican, he asserted the principles of Florentine esthetics.

B

ALDOVINETTI, Alessio. Italian School. Florence, 1425-1499. (Pages: 36, 46.)—A student and collaborator of Fra Angelico, he probably later entered the atelier of the engraver and goldsmith Maso Finiguerra. His works, executed with a complicated technique (a mixture of fresco, oil, and distemper painting), have been poorly preserved. He was adept at evoking not only fragile grace (*Madonna*, Louvre, Paris) but also monumental grandeur (*The Nativity*, Cloister of the Annunziata, Florence). He was one of the most abstract minds of Florence.

AYEU, Francisco. FRANCISCO BAYEU Y SUBIAS. Spanish School. 1734-1795. (Page: 287.)—Both a religious and profane decorator (the Cathedral of Toledo; the Pilar of Saragossa, 1775-1780), a portraitist without great personality, Bayeu showed his originality, with a typically Spanish grace, in his series of tapestry cartoons for the Santa Barbara factory. Brother-in-law of Goya, he came under his influence, as well as that of Mengs.

ELLINI, Giovanni. GIAMBELLINO. Italian School. Venice, about 1430-1516. (Pages: 46, 51, 54, 126, 131, 138, 150, 152.)—An illegitimate son of Jacopo Bellini, and brother of Gentile, he first underwent the influence of his father, and then was deeply affected by the art of his brother-in-law, Mantegna. About 1473, date at which he painted the *Coronation of the Virgin* at Pesaro, a great change is evidenced in the color and light which he uses to fashion space. Subsequently, Bellini painted both landscapes (*The Resurrection of Christ*, Berlin) and large altar pictures (Altar of San Giobbe). Also a decorator (lost frescoes of the Palace of the Doges) and a portraitist (*The Doge Loredano*), he opened the way to the next generation of painters by his last works (Altar of San Giovanni Crisostomo 1513); and it was almost symbolic that Titian should later finish Bellini's *Feast of the Gods* (Washington).

BERLINGHERI. Italian School. Lucca, about 1215-1240. (Pages: 23, 29.) —Cited in 1228 and mentioned as already dead in 1242. The name Berlinghieri, which is usually given him, is due to an error in the translation of a Latin document of 1228 which is known through certain 17th century transcriptions. The Crucifix of the picture gallery of Lucca, painted between 1210 and 1220, is signed: Berlingeri. Head of a school which during the 13th century at Lucca, interpreted the Byzantine tradition in an outstanding and personal manner, he not only formed his three sons Bonaventura, Marco, and Barone, but he strongly influenced numerous painters of Lucca, as well as Florentine and Pisan artists ot the first half of the 13th century.

BERMEJO, Bartolome. Spanish School. Second half of the 15th century (Pages: 114, 115.)—A native of Cordova, he signed his works "Vermejo" (*Pietà*, 1490, cathedral of Barcelona) or "Rubeus" (*St. Michael*, Ludlow Collection). He worked in Aragon as early as 1474, date of the *Altar piece of Santo Domingo* of Daroca (Prado). In 1486 he was in Catalonia and in 1498 at the cathedral of Vich. His monumental and powerful art asserts a typically Spanish realism, despite certain Flemish traits Bermejo's influence is dominant in Aragon at the end of the 15th century.

BLACKBURN, Joseph. American School. 1700-1765. (Pages : 299, 300, 302.)—Born in Connecticut, the son of a painter, his earliest works display a mature style that presumably was formed in England (where some historians also believe he was born). His main activity as a portraitist of well-to-do New Englanders was between 1753 and 1763. After this, he apparently left the country. There is a record of his having painted in Bermuda.

BOSCH, Jerome. HIERONYMUS VAN AEKEN. Flemish School. Died in 1516 (Pages: 59, 73, 74, 75, 174.)—He was undoubtedly born, between 1450 and 1460, at s'Hertogenbosch, from which he derived the name of Bosch Nothing is known of his formation, and even the chronology of his works is hypothetical, for lack of points of reference. He worked mainly at s'Hertogenbosch, where he died. He was a religious painter (*The Adoration of the Magi*, Prado, Madrid) and a moralist (*The Temptations*), but above all a visionary with a prodigious power of imagination. His fantasy is however based upon a scrupulous attention to reality, as revealed in his drawings. The strangeness of his visions is translated by bold stroke and clear, vivid coloring. Bosch's art inaugurated the representation of an imaginary world in which vice and the spirit of evil were stigmatized.

BOTTICELLI, Sandro. True name ALESSANDRO or SANDRO FILIPEPI. Italian School. Florence, 1444-1510. (Pages: 43, 44, 49, 55.)—At first a goldsmith, he entered the atelier of Fra Filippo Lippi whose influence he underwent, as well as that of Verrochio and Pollaiolo. As early as 1474 he was in the service of the Medici. His *Madonna of the Magnificat*, and his *Madonna of the Pomegranate* (Uffizi) are very representative of those graceful and melancholy compositions wherein he seeks decorative rhythms. Called to Rome by Sixtus IV, he painted a series of frescoes at the Sistine Chapel. The poems of Polliano inspired him to paint the *Allegory of Spring* and the *Birth of Venus* (Uffizi); and he attempted to reconstruct the *Calumny of Apelles* after the description of Lucian. Under the influence of Savonarola, he burned his pagan works, and henceforth his religious paintings were to reflect a violent mysticism (*The Entombment*, Munich). Botticelli formed Filippino Lippi and Lorenzo di Credi.

OUCHER, François. French School. 1703-1770. (Pages: 248, 250, 253, 259.)—A pupil of Lemoine and Cars, he was a boarding student at the Academy of France in Rome. A member of the Academy, later a professor, and finally its director, he was also appointed director of the Gobelins factory in 1753, and in 1765 First Painter to the King. He was principally a decorator, although he tried his hand at all types of painting: portraits, interior scenes, pastorals, and even religious compositions. His graceful, facile, and brilliant art is very representative of the Louis XV style.

OUTS, Albrecht. Flemish School. Died in 1458. (Page: 68.)—The second son of Dirk, and a painter like his brother whose work remains unknown, he worked and died at Louvain. He was a skilled popularizer of his father's works which, with his many students, he helped to diffuse.

OUTS, Dirk. Flemish School. Died in 1475. (Pages: 59, 65, 67, 85, 89.)— Born in Haarlem, perhaps about 1415-1420, he developed in his native city before going to Brussels to work next to Weyden. In 1457 he settled in Louvain where he was active until his death. His oldest dated work is a *Portrait of a Man* (1462, London). He differs from Rogier van der Weyden by a style which is more rigid but which retains a fine sincerity.

RÉA, Louis. French School. Died about 1522-1523. (Page: 110.)—One of the most outstanding representatives of the Brea family of Nice. His two sons, Antoine and François, also became painters. The art of Louis Bréa unites the monumental quality of Fouquet with a softened expression which comes from Lombardy (*Pietà*, 1475, Nice). He collaborated with Vincenzo Foppa in 1490.

RIL, Paul. Flemish School. 1554-1626. (Pages: 195, 200.)—A student of Damiaen Ortelmans and his brother Matthys, at Antwerp, Bril later went to Italy in 1574 and worked there until his death. In his frescoes (St. Cecilia of Transtevere, 1599) and in his easel paintings, he stresses composed landscapes, of which he was one of the initiators.

RONZINO. True name ANGIOLO DI COSIMO. Italian School. Florence, 1503-1572. (Pages: 132, 134, 135.)—A student and assistant of Pontormo, he worked at the Court of Urbino between 1530 and 1532. Later patronized by Cosimo de Medici, he painted mainly at Florence, executing portraits, mural decorations, and religious compositions (*Deposition*, Besançon). Influenced by Michelangelo, he is one of the most eminent representatives of Florentine mannerism, especially in his elegant and rigorous portraits (*Lucrezia Panchiatichi*, about 1540, Pitti).

BROUWER, Adriaen. Dutch School. 1605/1606-1638. (Page: 208.)— A
though the identity of his master is not known, his early works refle
the influence of Pieter Brueghel the Elder. In 1626 he was in Amsterda
and two years later at Haarlem in the studio of Frans Hals. It was aft
1631 that he settled in Antwerp, where he died some years later. His gen
scenes profoundly influenced Teniers' early works.

BRUEGHEL THE ELDER. Flemish School. About 1525-1569. (Page
174, 175, 179, 182, 183, 200.)—Born between 1520 and 1530, he spent h
apprenticeship with Peter Coecke. After his reception into the gild
Antwerp (1551), he left for Italy, and upon his return he established himse
at Antwerp where he made drawings for Jerome Cock (*The Proverbs*). H
painted works came at a later date. In 1563, he married Marie Coeck
the daughter of his master, and settled in Brussels. The year 1565 mar
the height of his genius, with *The Misanthropist* (Naples) and the seri
of the "*Months*." His overall conception of landscape anticipates t
baroque painters, while his naturalism links him with the preceding master
He sometimes seems to foreshadow the Rubens of *The Kermesse* (*Peasa
Dance*, Vienna), and he also continues the fantasy of the Gothics (*Trium*
of Death, Prado).

BRUEGHEL, Jan. Called VELVET BRUEGHEL. Flemish School. 1568-162
(Page: 201.)—The son of Pieter Brueghel the Elder, he was painter to t
Cardinal Federico Borromeo in Roma, and then to the Archduke Albert an
the Infanta Isabella in Brussels. He was closely attached to Rubens wh
had a high opinion of him, and both artists are known to have collaborate
(*The Earthly Paradise*, The Hague). A painter of flowers and landscap
his archaic and over-refined technique was imitated with success by h
son Jan II.

C

CANALETTO, ANTONIO DA CANALE. Italian School. Venice, 1697-176₈
(Pages: 188, 190, 193.)—Under the direction of his father Bernardo,
theater decorator, Canaletto became familiar with the art of perspectiv
and scenography. He made two trips to England (in 1746-1747, and agai
in 1751), and there he undoubtedly came under the influence of Van Heyde
who was in great favor. During his best period, from 1730 to 1746 (Lich
tenstein Collection, Dresden, London, and Paris), he excelled at renderin
the monumental aspects of Venice in warm and luminous tones.

CARAVAGGIO. True name MICHELANGELO MERISI. Italian School. Abou
1573-1609. (Pages: 187, 188, 189, 223, 226.)—His development followe
quite closely the examples of the Venetian masters of the Quattrocento an
the beginning of the Cinquecento. In 1589 he was at Rome working wit
the Cavalier d'Arpin and Prosperino delle Grotesche. But he soon brok
away, and, amidst enthusiasm and scandals, between 1590 and 1595, h
painted his stories of St. Matthew and St. Louis. The paintings fo
St. Mary of the People were executed from 1600 to 1601. His violent an
poverty-stricken existence was to terminate tragically at Porto d'Ercol
in 1609. His art reacted vigorously against the official pompous style o
the time. He utilized the resources of chiaroscuro to create a dramati

atmosphere, and by his popular types, his genre pictures, and his still-lifes he greatly influenced Italian, Spanish, and French painting of the 17th century.

CARON, Antoine. French School. About 1520-1598. (Pages: 144, 147.)—Born in Beauvais, he developed at Fontainebleau where the records report him between 1540 and 1550, and again in 1560. He painted the triumphal entry of Charles IX in 1569, and that of the Duke of Anjou in 1573, when the latter was elected King of Poland. Caron had been appointed painter and draughtsman to the King in 1572. His painted works are very characteristic of the mannerism of the School of Fontainebleau (*Augustus and the Sibylle*, Louvre). He produced the cartoons for the tapestry of the *Story of Artemesia*.

CARPACCIO, Vittore. Italian School. Venice. Died in 1527. (Page: 52.)—A student and disciple of Gentile Bellini, he also underwent the influence of Antonello da Messina and the Flemish painters. Information on his activity dates back to 1486. He worked a great deal for the religious brotherhoods of Venice, decorating their monasteries, in the manner of Gentile, with great narrative cycles of which the most perfect is the *Cycle of St. Ursula* (1490-1496, Academy of Venice). Between 1502 and 1510 he executed the decorations of San Giorgio dei Schiavoni. His adventurous imagination mingled Venice with the Orient. He was also one of the most sensitive landscape artists of his time.

CARRACCI, Annibale. Italian School. Bologna, 1560-1609. (Pages: 185, 186, 187, 188.)—He developed under the direction of his cousin, Ludovico Carracci (1555-1619). In 1585, Ludovico, Annibale and his brother Agostino (1557-1602) opened the Academy of the Desiderosi whose eclectic program aimed at putting a stop to the mediocrity of artistic studies by following the examples of the great masters. Annibale, who was influenced by Corregio, Titian, and Veronese, left a great variety of works. A landscape artist (*The Flight into Egypt*, Doria Gallery, Rome), a realist (*The Eater of Beans*, Colonna Gallery, Rome), and a religious painter (*Virgin in Glory*, Bologna), he was also a skilful decorator who, in the frescoes of the Farnese Palace at Rome, gave the model for decorative painting of his time. The influence of the Carracci, who founded the Bolognese School of Painting, was considerable in Italy and France in the 17th century.

CASTAGNO, Andrea del. Italian School. Florence, 1390(?)-1457. (Pages: 36, 41, 46.)—In 1442 he decorated the San Tarasio Chapel at San Zaccaria of Venice, and he also probably executed certain mosaics at San Marco. His *Assumption* (1449, Berlin), and his *Niccolo da Tolentino* (1455, Dome of Florence) are very characteristic of his voluntary art which attempts to give the illusion of sculpture. His last work, *The Lord's Supper* (refectory of the hospital of Santa Maria Novella) is both powerful and abstract; it was executed shortly before the artist died of the plague.

CHAMPAIGNE, Philippe de. French School. 1602-1674. (Pages: 237, 238, 241, 242.)—Born in Brussels, a student of Bouillon and Fouquières, he went to Paris in 1621 and worked on the decoration of the Luxembourg Palace. He was painter to Marie de Medici, and later to the King. A religious painter (*Adoration of the Shepherds*, Wallace Collection, London), and a remarkable portraitist (*Richelieu*, Louvre), his style attains an austere grandeur in his portraits of the Jansenists (*Ex Voto*, 1662, Louvre).

CHARDIN, Jean-Baptiste-Siméon. French School. 1699-1779. (Pages: 2 253, 263, 264.)—A student of Cazes, he was so greatly influenced by Flemish and Dutch masters that his early works, *The Ray* and *The Bu* (Louvre), which were noticed by Largillière at the exposition of yo painters, were taken for Flemish paintings. He was accepted by Academy in 1728, and in 1755 he became its treasurer. He painted ge scenes characterized by their intimate quality (*The Grace*, Louvre), and known especially for his still-lifes. He also painted door designs for chateaux of Choisy and Bellevue. At the end of his life, his failing vis forced him to employ pastels, which he handled with surprising keenn (*Self Portrait*, Louvre).

CHRISTUS, Petrus. Flemish School. Died in 1472. (Page: 61.)—A nat of Baerle, and probably a student of Jan van Eyck at Bruges, where obtained his Mastership in 1441, he apparently worked in the latter c until his death in 1472. His dated works are situated between 1446 a 1457. A portraitist and religious painter, his works of lasting value rev the influence of the Van Eycks and Van der Weyden (Diptych of Berl 1452).

CIMABUE. CENNO DI PEPO or PEPE. Florentine School. Florence, mention from 1272 to 1302. (Pages: 25, 32.)—In a document dated 1302, he mentioned as the author of a *Saint John* in a mosaic of the Cathedral Pisa; by analogy with the style of that work, one may also ascribe to hi with certainty, the *Madonna of the Santa Trinita* (Uffizi, Florence) and c tain frescoes of the Upper Basilica (vaulting and walls of the choir) and t Lower Basilica of Assisi (*Madonna with St. Francis*). He went to Ro in 1272 and there he undoubtedly met Cavallini who helped free him fr the Byzantine masters to whom he owed the type and technique of painting. In his work, the memory of the grandeur of Byzantium ming with an entirely new and more human softness.

CLERCK, Hendrik de. Flemish School. 1570-1629. (Page: 201.)—Bo and probably died in Brussels. He was a pupil of Martin de Vos Antwerp, and later painted mainly for the churches of his birth-pla frequently in collaboration with other artists.

CLOUET, François. French School. About 1516-1572. (Page: 149.)— Bo in Tours, the son of Jean Clouet; upon the death of his father, François i herited his titles of valet and painter to the King. He painted myth logical compositions (*The Bath of Diana*, Rouen), but mainly portra (*The Botanist Pierre Cuthe*, 1562, Louvre) which were preceded by pen drawings of an authority and grace greatly imitated in France.

CLOUET, Jean. French School. About 1485-1540. (Pages: 145, 147, 14 149, 237, 261.)—Undoubtedly of Flemish origin, settled in Tours as ea as 1516, then in Paris in 1529, he was "painter and valet to the Kin under Louis XII and Francis I. He illustrated the Gallic Wars in mini tures, and principally painted and drew a great number of portraits.

COPLEY, John Singleton. American School. 1737-1815. (Pages: 300, 30 305.)—Born near Boston of Irish parents, his first master was his stepfath Peter Belham. A meticulous worker, he soon built up a solid cliente among the Boston elite. The Revolution found him in England associate through his wife's family, with the Tory sympathizers. Here he remaine taking on prevailing English style, enjoying financial success. Besides his portraits, the English period includes conversation pieces, historical scenes and religious paintings.

ORREGGIO, True name ANTONIO ALLEGRI. Italian School. Parma, 1494-1534. (Pages: 131, 132.)—His development is not known with any certainty, however his early works show the influence of Mantegna and Da Vinci. In 1516 he was in Parma; in 1518 he executed frescoes for the Camera di San Paolo, and shortly thereafter painted the *St. Catherine* of the Louvre. He was a prodigious painter of domes (between 1520 and 1530, St. John's and the Dome) where he opens perspectives on the Heavens and depicts strikingly foreshortened figures. All the baroque Italian painters of ceilings and vaulting took their inspiration from him. A painter of mythology (*Antiope*, Louvre; *Danaë*, Borghese Gallery, Rome), his gracefully sensual art was to influence the painters of the 18th century.

RANACH, Lucas. German School. 1472-1553. (Pages: 156, 159, 160.)—His real name was Lucas Sender or Maler. He undoubtedly developed in the studio of his father who was also a painter. In 1505 he established himself at Wittenberg, the seat of the Court of Saxony, and until his death he was in the service of the Electors, executing numerous commissions. In addition he was occupied with public and private duties, and directed an atelier with the assistance of his sons, Hans (died 1537) and Lucas the Younger (died 1586). His personal works between 1525 and 1547 are not easily distinguished from secondary production. The biblical themes of that period (*Samson and Delilah*, Augsburg) are closely allied with mythological themes, often of erotic inspiration (*The Fountain of Youth*, Berlin). A painter of animals (*Hunts*, Vienna and Madrid), and a portraitist (*Double Portrait*, Reinhart Collection, Winterthur), his production was disseminated by his studio and enjoyed a great popularity.

CUYP, Albert. Dutch School. 1620-1691. (Page: 212.)—Born at Dordrecht. A peace-loving and healthy nature, with a taste for large, well-balanced pictures. He excelled equally in rustic scenes and in the depicting of wealthy townsfolk. Among his finest works may be mentioned: *The Walk, The Grey and White Horses*, and likewise a *View of Dordrecht*.

D

DAVID, Gerard. Flemish School. About 1460-1523. (Pages: 166, 167, 171.)—Probably born at Oudewater, near Utrecht, he is known to have been a member of the corporation of painters at Bruges in 1484. He sojourned temporarily in Antwerp (1515), but lived mainly in Bruges, where he died. With Memling, he was one of the finest painters of the School of Bruges at the end of the 15th century (*The Madonna with Saints*, 1509, Rouen).

DESPORTES, François. French School. 1661-1743. (Page: 252.)—He arrived in Paris in 1678 and later was called to Poland by John Sobieski. Upon his return to France in 1696, he abandoned his career as portraitist to become a painter of animals. He depicted in particular the staghounds of Louis XIV and Louis XV. He also produced tapestry cartoons, and his landscape studies (Compiègne) reveal a very fine sensibility.

DOBSON, Sir William. English School. 1610-1646. (Pages: 273, 277.)—
He was formed by Robert Peake, painter to Charles I, and then worked
in the studio of Van Dyck who greatly influenced him (*Endymion Porte*
London).

DUCCIO DI BUONINSEGNA. Italian School. Siena, about 1260-about
1319. (Page: 28.)—He is known to have been active at Siena as early
as 1278. Obliged to flee to Florence after a serious sentence in 1285, he
may have painted the *"Rucellai" Madonna* about that same date. Between 1308 and 1311, he worked on the *Maestà* of the large altar of the Dom
at Siena. The influence of Byzantine painting, evident in his technique
modeling, chromatism, and iconography, joins with a linear harmony of
Gothic origin. Founder of the Sienese School, Duccio left his mark on
painting for an entire century.

DURER, Albrecht. German School. 1471-1528. (Pages: 54, 81, 89, 151, 152
153, 154, 155, 156, 165, 166.)—The son of a goldsmith of Hungarian origin
living in Nuremberg, Dürer entered the atelier of Wolgemut in 1486. He
undoubtedly made an initial trip to Venice around 1494-1495, immediately
after his marriage. Upon his return to Nuremberg he opened an atelier
his painting of that period shows the influence of his engraving, a medium
in which he produced incomparable masterpieces (*Apocalypse*, 1498). His
second trip to Italy (between 1505 and 1507) caused him to continue his
research of harmony and composition in the Venetian manner (*Adam an*
Eve, 1507, Prado; *Adoration of the Holy Trinity*, 1511, Vienna). The
greater part of his time was spent in engraving and wood-cutting (*Greater*
and Lesser Passion, 1510-1512; *Melancholie*). Highly renowned, a friend
of Pirkheimer, in the service of Maximilien, he traveled in the Low Countries, painting his last great work in 1526: *The Four Apostles* (Munich)
Taken ill, near the end of his life he gave a résumé of his research in
theoretical writings. Dürer provided the most beautiful, complex, and
profound expression of the German Renaissance.

F

FEKE, Robert. American School. 1705-1750. (Pages: 293, 300.)—Born
Oyster Bay, Long Island, son of a minister, he is believed to have gone
abroad about 1732 for nine years' study in Italy and Spain. 1741 settled
in Newport, Rhode Island, where he painted one of first American group
portraits. Artist later worked in Philadelphia, New York and Boston
Went to sea 1750 and died on a trip to the West Indies.

FOUQUET, Jean. French School. About 1420-1480. (Pages: 93, 95, 102, 103.
—Nothing is known of his formation, except that between 1443 and 1447
he went to Italy, and that at Rome he painted the portrait of Eugenius IV
accompanied by two members of his entourage. He returned to Tours
in 1448 at the latest. The King, the chancellor Juvenal des Ursins, and
Étienne Chevalier commissioned him to do portraits. In addition, he was
a miniaturist, a fresco painter, and vested with projects for funeral monuments, stained-glass windows, etc. He became the First Painter to King
Louis XI in 1475. His two sons, Louis and François, worked with him in

directing a very prosperous atelier which strongly influenced the entire valley of the Loire and even Paris. Only very few painted works and a certain number of miniatures are ascribed to him. His monumental style, of serene simplicity, is the most beautiful expression of French art in the 15th century.

RAGONARD, Jean-Honoré. French School. 1732-1806. (Pages: 253, 260, 265.)—He entered the atelier of Chardin, spent some time in Boucher's studio, was for three years a pupil of the "École des Élèves Protégés," and finished his instruction at Rome where he assimilated the most varied influences with extraordinary versatility. He soon concentrated on genre painting, sometimes of a decorative nature. His compositions (*The Bathers*, Louvre), his landscapes (*The Fête of St. Cloud*, Banque de France), and his portraits (*The Abbé St. Non*, Louvre) are less prized for their subject or their faithfulness to the model than for their nervous and admirably versatile execution. Named a member of the Jury of Arts in 1794, then a member of the Conservatory of the Museum, he was expelled in 1806 and died in great poverty.

RANCESCA, Piero Della. Italian School. Umbria, 1416-1492. (Pages: 36, 40, 44.)—Born in Borgo San Sepulcro, he early associated himself with Domenico Veneziano at Florence. The polyptych of the Brothers of Mercy of Borgo di San Sepulcro (1445) reveals the influence of Sassetta. In 1449 he painted frescoes at the Este Castle in Ferrara which strongly impressed the Ferrarese masters (Tura, Cossa). *The History of the True Cross* at San Francesco of Arezzo, executed between 1452 and 1453, is the high point of his art, along with the diptych of the Uffizi (about 1465, for Federigo da Montefeltro and Battista Sforza). Only fragments of his works remain at Rome, where he was called in 1459. With his scientific mind, fascinated by perspective and geometry, he wrote two theoretical treatises. His monumental art of majestic simplicity is one of the highest expressions of the Italian Renaissance.

FRIES, Hans. Swiss School. About 1465-after 1518. (Page: 158.)—A native of Freiburg where he was the municipal painter, Fries was an artist of transition between the style of the 15th century and that of the Reformation. His masterpiece is the double panel of Zurich which represents the two visions of St. John the Evangelist.

FROMENT, Nicolas. French School. Mentioned from 1450 to 1490. (Pages: 93, 98.)—Born at Uzès, he undoubtedly developed under a painter from the Low Countries settled in Provence, for a Dutch influence is very evident in his works: *The Resurrection of Lazarus* (1461, Uffizi, Florence); and his masterpiece, the *Triptych of the Burning Bush* (1475-1476, St. Sauveur Cathedral, Aix). Vigor and grandeur, and an insistent search for expression in his portraits, are characteristic of his manner and re-encountered in his school.

GADDI, Taddeo. Italian School. Florence, Died in 1366. (Pages: 27, 28.)— A student of Giotto, his oldest dated work is the triptych of the Kaiser Friedrich Museum (1334). He worked at San Miniato al Monte (1341-1342), at San Francesco, at Pisa, and in 1353 completed an altar painting for San Giovanni Fuorcivita at Pistoia. His best work is the decoration of the Baroncelli Chapel at the Santa Croce of Florence.

GAINSBOROUGH, Thomas. English School. 1727-1788. (Pages: 200, 2[?] 271, 277, 279, 281, 285.)—Born in Suffolk, he worked first in London wi[?] Gravelo, and then with Francis Hayman; in 1748 he settled at Bath. [?] was a member of the Royal Academy. His portraits are full of tenderne[?] and spontaneity (*The Painter's Daughters*, London), and they are a[?] romantic in their harmonious accord between personage and landscape.

GENTILE DA FABRIANO. Italian School. Province of the March[?] 1360-1427. (Pages: 27, 50.)—Born at Fabriano, in the Marches. In 14[?] he decorated the Council Hall of the Palace of the Doges at Venice. 1422, a member of the corporation of painters in Florence, he painted t[?] *Adoration of the Magi* (Uffizi) for the Church of the Trinity. A wanderi[?] painter, his narrative style, clear coloring, and softened modeling great[?] influenced the Venetians.

GHIRLANDAIO, Domenico Bigordi. Italian School. Florence, 1449-149[?] (Pages: 43, 51, 97.)—Formed in the atelier of Baldovinetti, he soon becam[?] a skilful decorator noted for his well ordered compositions full of a profa[?] picturesqueness (Santa Fina Chapel at San Gimignano, and the Sistir[?] Chapel, Rome, 1475; Sassetti Chapel at Santa Trinita of Florence, 148[?] Choir of Santa Maria Novella, Florence, 1486-1490). He had Michelange[?] as a student, and his atelier had a great importance in Florence.

GIORGIONE. GIORGIO DA CASTELFRANCO. Italian School. Venice, abo[?] 1477-1510. (Pages: 126, 131, 137, 138, 139, 201.)—His life and wo[?] remain very obscure. He went to Venice about 1495 and developed in th[?] environment of the Bellinis. He even exerted such an influence on th[?] elder Bellini and on Titian's early period that their works have often bee[?] confused. Unfortunately, nothing remains of his decorations (Fondacc[?] dei Tedeschi, with Titian). His easel paintings (*Madonna of Castelfranc[?] The Three Philosophers*, Vienna; *The Tempest* and *The Old Woman*, Venice[?] *The Sleep of Venus*, Dresden; *The Concert in the Open Air*, Louvre) renewe[?] the Venetian inspiration and technique by a mastery of color and ligh[?] effects. His influence was considerable on the development of Venetia[?] painting.

GIOTTO. True name AMBROGIO DI BONDONE. Italian School. Florence[?] about 1266-1337. (Pages: 23, 25, 26, 27, 28, 30, 36, 40, 115.)—He worke[?] on the Upper Basilica at Assisi between 1296 and 1304 (*Life of St. Francis* and later, if one accepts the affirmation of Ghiberti, on the "*Franciscan Allegories*" in the Chapel of the Magdalen of the Lower Basilica. Thi[?] student of Cimbue, according to Vasari, breaks definitely with th[?] Byzantine tradition. His art asserts itself in the Arena Chapel at Padu[?] (*Scenes from the life of Christ and the Virgin*, painted, before 1305, for Enric[?] Scrovengi). Of his Florentine works, there remain the chapels of Bard[?] (*Stories of St. Francis*, after 1317) and Peruzzi (*Stories of St. John*) a[?] Santa Croce. Highly original in his human inspiration and in his dramatic style of noble simplicity, he was the founder of the Florentine School.

GONÇALVES, Nuño. Portuguese School. Second half of the 15th century. (Pages: 115, 116.)—A Portuguese painter, in the service of Alfonso the[?] African in 1463, he assimilated in a very personal manner the Flemish[?]

influence which was very strong in Portugal in the 15th century. Typical of his style are the two triptychs of *St. Vincent* at the museum of Lisbon. By analogy, the technique and the quality of the portraits have caused him to be credited with *The Man with the Wine Glass* (Louvre) and the *Portrait of a Man* (Lichtenstein Collection, Vienna).

OSSART, Jan. Called MABUSE. Flemish School. Died between 1533 and 1536. (Pages: 166, 168, 172.)—He was enrolled (1503) in the corporation of painters at Antwerp under the name of Gennyn du Hainaut. He was later surnamed Van Mabuse, after the Flemish form for the town of "Maubeuge." He was in the service of Philip of Burgundy (in Italy, 1508; at Middleburg, 1509; and at Utrecht, 1517); he also served Margaret of Austria. He died between 1533 and 1536. His work shows Italian tendencies, but he retains the frankness and the perfection of treatment characteristic of the Flemish School.

OYA, Francisco-José. FRANCISCO GOYA Y LUCIENTES. Spanish School. 1746-1828. (Pages: 188, 227, 269, 287, 289, 290, 291, 292.)—At Saragossa he frequented the studio of Martinez Luzan. In 1775, Bayeu had him engaged in the group of Mengs for the tapestry factory of Santa Barbara, and Goya worked there until 1791. Painter to the Camara, a close friend of the Albas and the Osonas, he concentrated on portraits of the Royal Family. In 1792, stricken with deafness, his misanthropy and isolation spurred him on to a more and more fierce and visionary art (*The Caprices*). This tendency became further accentuated under the influence of Spain's misfortunes, of which Goya gives a harrowing vision in his engravings (*The Disasters of War*). In 1814, in the service of Ferdinand VII, he painted realistic scenes and some of his finest works: *The Second and Third of May* (Prado). Withdrawn to France in 1824, he died there four years later. His bold technique, his universal inspiration, and his entire work, which included all types of painting, left a deep impression upon Spain and France in the 19th century.

GOZZOLI, Benozzo. Italian School. Florence, 1424-1497. (Pages: 36, 43, 50.)—The favorite student and collaborator of Fra Angelico, he took his inspiration from his master as well as from Gentile da Fabriano, and later underwent the influence of Lippi and Botticelli. He was a prolific decorator (*Life of St. Francis* at San Francesco de Montefalco, 1450-1452; *Life of St. Augustine* at San Agostino de San Gimignano, 1463-1467; *Cycle of the Old Testament* at the Campo Santo of Pisa, 1468-1485). His most famous work is the *Procession of the Magi* of the Riccardi Palace (1459-1461) in which he takes his inspiration from the procession of the Emperor of Byzantium, John VII Palaeologus, arriving at the council of Florence.

GRECO, EL DOMENICO THEOTOCOPULI. Spanish School. 1541-1614. (Pages: 165, 223, 224, 225, 227, 228, 229, 231, 287, 289.)—Born on the island of Crete, he undoubtedly first learned to paint according to Byzantine techniques. Toward 1560 he went to Venice and profited from the examples of Bassano and Titian; but if he appropriated the manner of the Venetians, his talent of that period remained highly original. From 1570 to 1572(?) he was in Rome, a close friend of Giulio Clovio of whom he left a handsome portrait (Naples). He left Italy suddenly for Spain, working at Toledo in

1577. His works, which are strange because of their mysticism and bo
technique, are sometimes disconcerting (*Espolio*, Munich; *Martyrdom
St. Maurice*, Escorial). His is a visionary art (*The Burial of Count Orga*
Toledo) whose lyricism attains an extraordinary intensity in the last wor
of the master (*Vision of the Apocalypse*).

GRIEN, Hans Baldung. German School. About 1484-1545. (Page: 16)
—Surnamed Grien (adjective form of "grün": green) because of his predile
tion for that color. Undoubtedly of Swabian origin, and from a family
scholars and humanists, he liked mythological themes and especially nud
(*Pyramus and Thisbe*, Berlin) which he frequently represented in fantast
scenes, with a striking expressionism. (*The Kiss of Death*, Basel.)

GRUNEWALD, Mathias. German School. About 1455/1460-1528. (Page
163, 165.)—The name of "Grünewald" was supposedly invented by San
rart (Deutsche Akademie, 1675), and the painter to whom it refe
should be identified with Mathis Gothardt Nithardt (or Neidthard
an artist and engineer born in Auschaffenburg around 1455 or 146
He was probably a pupil of Master E.S. at Strasbourg, and then
Schongauer at Colmar. After 1508, he was court painter, artistic cou
cillor, and Archbishop of Mayence. Between 1512 and 1515 he pain
ed his masterpiece, the altar-piece of the church of Isenheim (Colmar
In 1525 he lost his position and sought refuge in Frankfurt, and later i
Halle where he worked on hydraulic projects before his death in 1528
His strange work, extraordinarily bold in conception and technique, mad
him one of the greatest masters of German painting.

GUARDI, Francesco. Italian School. Venice, 1712-1793. (Pages: 188, 193)
—He began his study of painting under his brother, Gianantonio, wit
whom he collaborated closely until the latter's death in 1760. He owe
a great deal to Maffei, Bazzani, the Ricci, and Magnasco. At firs
a painter of figures (*Il Ridotto, Ca' Rezzonico*, Venice), he concentrate
more and more on the painting of landscapes, which he depicts luminousl
and with a vibrant touch. All documentary or narrative characte
disappears in favor of an extremely free poetic sensibility.

GUERCINO. True name GIOVANNI FRANCESCO BARBIERI. Italian School
Bologna, 1591-1666. (Pages: 187, 188.)—A pupil of Benedetto Gennar
at Cento, and then of Ludovico Carracci at Bologna, his first works, ii
which he utilizes the resources of chiaroscuro, are undoubtedly his fines
(*St. Peter Resuscitating Tabitha*, 1618, Pitti). But his admiration fo
Caravaggio soon gave way to the influence of the Roman School and tc
that of Guido Reni; his art then became academic and cold. He wa
one of the most individualistic draughtsmen of the Bolognese School.

GUIDO DA SIENA. Italian School. Siena, 13th century. (Pages: 24, 28.)
—Known solely through the inscription and the date 1221 (sometimes
interpreted 1271) of a Madonna of the Palazzo Pubblico at Siena, Guido has
been variously identified with Guido di Ghezzo or Guido di Graziano.
He was, before Duccio, the most important master of Siena in the second
half of the 13th century. The numerous works showing signs of his
manner prove that he directed an important atelier. He had, for example,
a great influence on certain Tuscan masters (Coppo di Marcovaldo).

H

ALS, Frans. Dutch School. 1580-1666. (Pages: 208, 211, 215.)—A student of Karel Van Mander in Haarlem before 1603, he remained in that city until his death. In 1617-1618, he figured among the honorary members of the Society of Rhetoric. In 1644 he was the head of the Gild of St. Lucas, but, leading an irregular life, he was dogged by misery and finished his days in an Old People's Home. He painted admirable collective portraits (*The "Regents" of the Old Men's Home*, 1641, Haarlem), and also plebeian figures showing a nervous stroke that attempts to render the fugitive.

ERRERA THE ELDER, Francisco. Spanish School. 1576-1656. (Pages: 222, 223, 227.)—Born in Seville where be worked almost all of his life. The school of Seville owes him a new development and technique based on freedom and courage. He set before himself grandiose and magnificent ideals. Masses of light and color in audacious contrats. He died in Madrid leaving a profound influence in the art of Spain.

ESSELIUS, Gustavus. American School. 1682-1785. (Pages: 296, 298.) —Born Falun, Sweden, trained in Stockholm where, thanks to many foreign artists, he acquired their international style. Came to America in 1712, settling first in Philadelphia, later in Annapolis where he developed a clientele among the Maryland families. A maker of musical instruments, he built the first pipe organ in America in Bethlehem, Pa.

OGARTH, William. English School. 1697-1764. (Pages: 269, 270, 274, 275.)—He began his career working for a goldsmith, then turned to picture engraving. He worked in the studio of the painter Thornhill, who became his father-in-law. After 1731, he produced his best known works which he subsequently engraved. Interested by esthetics, he published a theoretical essay in 1753 ("Analysis of Beauty"). He became painter to the King in 1757. He was an animated and waggish painter of the mores of his time.

OLBEIN, Hans. German School. About 1497/1498-1543. (Pages: 54, 151, 152, 153, 156, 162, 164, 165, 166, 267.)—Born in Augsburg, he was formed by his father Holbein the Elder. In 1515 he was in Basel, with his friends Erasmus and Amerbach. He undoubtedly went to Italy before 1518, for the influence of the School of Da Vinci is perceptible in his early works. Having returned to Basel in 1518, he married there and executed numerous decorative works. It was then that he painted his most beautiful religious compositions (*The Dead Christ*, Basel) and the portraits of *Erasmus* and *Boniface Amerbach*. His talent as a portraitist established itself even more firmly during his sojourns in London (between 1526 and 1528; 1532 and 1543) (*Nicholas Kratzer*, Louvre; *George Gysen*, Berlin), and for eleven years he was the favorite painter of Henry VIII. Holbein's drawings reveal by what admirable simplicity of expression he arrived at the rigorous and faithful style of his portraits.

IOOGH, Pieter de. Dutch School. 1629-after 1683. (Pages: 208, 219.)— He worked in Delft about 1653, then until 1657 at Leyden and The Hague. He is known to have settled in Amsterdam before 1668. A student of Berchem, he was a genre painter and a particularly refined craftsman, with an exquisite sensibility for lighting effects.

J

JORDAENS, Jacob. Flemish School. 1593-1678. (Page: 202.)—He w
a pupil of Adam Van Noort, and later married Van Noort's daught
He worked at Antwerp; and, if he did not make the journey to Italy,
did at least come in contact with the followers of Caravaggio who influenc
his early works (*The Satyr* and *Peasant*, Cassel). A robust painter
compositions are full of Flemish wholesomeness and the joy of livi
(*The King Drinks*, Brussels). After the death of Rubens, Jordae
completed the decoration of the Torre de la Parada.

K

KUHN, Justus Engelhardt. American School. Active between 1708-171
(Page 296.)—This artist, who was born in Germany, worked in Ameri
between 1708 and 1717. He painted members of old families in Maryla
to whom he lent a ffattering sir of refinement. His own life bears w
ness to this same quality. He died in America.

L

LANCRET, Bernard. French School. 1690-1743. (Pages: 248, 257.)
A student of Dulin, and then of Gillot, he followed Watteau's counsel I
painting landscapes and figures from Nature. Admitted to the Acaden
in 1719, he painted "gallant" scenes in the manner of Watteau, and subje
pictures full of animation (*The Luncheon*, Chantilly). He also execute
decorations for Versailles, Fontainebleau, and la Muette.

LARGILLIÈRE, Nicholas de. French School. 1656-1746. (Pages: 24
256.)—He was formed by Goebouw at Antwerp. In 1674 he was
London and collaborated with Lely. Academician in 1686, he becam
a professor at the Academy in 1705. He executed numerous collectiv
portraits which have not all survived. His models were most often take
from the bourgeoisie. He was a magnificent technician (*The Belle Stra
bourgeoise*, Sassoon Collection).

LA TOUR, Georges de. French School. Died in 1652. (Pages: 147, 23
236.)—A native of Lorraine, born at Vic, he probably settled in Lunévil
shortly before his marriage. He undoubtedly traveled in Italy an
went to Rome before 1613, for his works prove that he knew the Roma
Caravaggesque environment; perhaps he also went to Holland where h
may have seen the disciples of Caravaggio. The name of Dumesn
(Duménil), which was given him, belonged in reality to his son Étienne
The chronology of his works is uncertain: he painted religious scenes an
genre pictures in the manner of the disciples of Caravaggio. In 164
Painter-in-Ordinary to the King, he became famous principally throug
his "Nights" (*The New-born Infant*, Rennes), but he also treated day
light scenes which have sometimes been ascribed to Spanish master
(*The Hurdy-gurdy Player*, Rouen).

LA TOUR, Maurice Quentin de. French School. 1704-1788. (Pages: 147
251, 261, 264.)—Pastellist, pupil of Spoède and Dupuch, he was know
for his talent and his extravagant temperament. He bequeathed to hi

native town of St. Quentin a large number of his paintings and almost all of his admirable preparations. He left a dazzling gallery of the society of the time of Louis XV.

E BRUN, Charles. French School. 1619-1690. (Pages: 237, 240, 244.)—A student of Perrier and Vouet, noted by Richelieu and Séguier, he left for Rome in 1642. Upon his return, in 1646, he was patronized by Fouquet and then by Colbert. Secretary of the Academy, he was named First Painter to the King in 1662, and director of the Royal Gobelins factory. He exerted a veritable dictatorial control on the art of his time. The decorations of Versailles are full of that spirit of ostentation and grandeur which characterized art under Louis XIV. Le Brun was also a remarkable portraitist (*The Chancellor Séguier*, Louvre).

ELY, Peter. English School. 1618-1680. (Pages: 269, 270, 302.)—Born in Westphalia, he went to England about 1641. He was strongly influenced by the art of Van Dyck. His famous atelier formed numerous painters: Gerard Soest, Kneller, etc.

E NAIN, Louis. Frrench School. 1593-1645. (Pages: 240, 243.)—He was formed by his brother Antoine (1593[?]-1645) who, about 1630, opened a studio in Paris in collaboration with his young brother Matthieu (1607-1677). All three were members of the Academy. Their works, which were formerly confused, are now able to be distinguished. Antoine, the most Flemish, was the author of small bourgeois and rustic scenes characterized by a savory awkwardness and minute attention to detail. Whereas Matthieu liked elegant or mythological scenes, Louis preferably painted peasants, with a spirit full of dignity (*The Peasants' Meal*, Louvre). None of the humorous, rustic bambocciade remains in his art: he elevated genre pictures to a higher level.

HE LIMBURG BROTHERS. Franco-Flemish School. First half of the 15th century. (Pages: 20, 21, 22.)—Of Flemish origin, probably the nephews of the painter Jean Malouel, the brothers were also named Malouel. They were first in the service of John the Fearless and Philip the Bold, and later painted for the Duke of Berry. Pol de Limburg (died shortly after 1416) and his two brothers, Jan and Hennequin (died before 1434) painted the *Very Rich Hours of the Duke of Berry*, a masterpiece of Franco-Flemish painting. One of the most active centers of this school was the Court of Dijon.

LIPPI, Fra Filippo. Italian School. Florence, 1406-1469. (Pages: 36, 39, 43.)—He entered the Monastery of the Carmelites in 1421, led an adventurous life, and in 1437 had a son, Filippino, in an affair with a young nun, Lucrezia Buti. At first responsive to the grace of Gentile da Fabriano and Angelico, he soon became interested in the problems of representing volumes (*The Virgin and Saints*, Louvre, Paris); and, mainly under the influence of Masaccio (*Coronation of the Virgin*, Uffizi, Florence), he decorated the Cathedrals of Prato and Spoleto during the last years of his life. He was one of the first to introduce a secular spirit into religious painting.

LOCHNER, Stephan. German School. Died in 1451. (Pages: 81, 85, 87.)—He was probably born between 1405 and 1415 at Meersburg, on the Lake of Constance. No trace of his activity has been found outside

the city of Cologne whose pleasantness and grace his work so well express
His inspiration is unusually fresh in the altar-piece of *The Last Judgm*
(Cologne, Frankfurt-on-the-Main, Munich) and in the Dombild (Cathed
of Cologne). There is an amiable religiosity in his last and only dat
work, *The Presentation in the Temple* (1447, Darmstadt).

LORENZETTI, Ambroglio. Italian School. Siena. Died in 1348. (Pag
30.)—Younger brother of Pietro Lorenzetti, perhaps killed with hi
during the plague of 1348. The first mention of Ambrogio dates fro
1319. His masterpiece is the decoration of the Council Room of t
Public Palace of Siena (1337-1339), in which he humanizes the allegor
The *Effects of Good Government* are placed amidst vast and impressi
panoramic landscapes. Ambrogio's style unites the monumental quali
of Giotto with the characteristic grace of the Sienese School.

LORRAIN, Claude. CLAUDE GELLÉE, called LE LORRAIN. French Schoo
1600-1682. (Pages: 240, 246, 276.)—Born at Champagne, in Lorrain
he was first a pastry maker and servant before becoming the pupil of th
landscape artist Tassi. He began to paint in Rome about 1620, and h
remained there permanently, except for one brief sojourn in Franc
After his early canvases which were quite realistic, he devoted himself t
the type of painting which was to bring his success: sea ports, and countr
sides transfigured by magnificent lighting effects. He was one of th
greatest landscape painters of the French School and his sensibility an
lyricism announce the modern masters.

LUCAS VAN LEYDEN. Flemish School. 1494-1533. (Pages: 166, 181.)—
Student of his father, Huygh Jacobsz, and of Cornelis Engelbrechtser
An engraver, he is known to have had contact with Dürer. By his genr
pictures and his luminism, he announces certain effects of Dutch painting

LUINI, Bernardino. Italian School. Milan, about 1480-1532. (Page: 123.
—If he was not a student of Da Vinci, he at least profited from his advic
and example. He was a prolific and graceful fresco painter (Villa Pelucca
1507; Santa Maria della Pace, Milan, 1521; Saronno, 1525; Monaster
Maggiore, Milan, 1526; Saint Mary of the Angels, Lugano, 1529). Hi
canvases, fewer in number, recall Da Vinci by their technique, thei
inspiration, and their search for gentle softness.

M

MANTEGNA, Andrea. Italian School. Padua, 1432-1506. (Pages: 53, 54
88, 92, 166.)—Adopted by Squarcione, who seems to have been a sor
of clever contractor rather than the innovating painter he had formerly
been considered, Mantegna perhaps learned from him the appreciation
of antique beauty. Mantegna's contact with Donatello at the Santo o
Padua served to complete the revelation of the artist to himself (*Story*
of St. James and St. Christopher, Eremitani, Padua, 1449-1454). From 1457
to 1459 he painted the large altar-piece of San Zeno (Verona). Settled
in Mantua in 1468, he remained there, in the service of Isabella d'Este
and the Gonzague family, until his death. He decorated the castle (Camera
degli Sposi, 1468 to 1474) and the *Studiolo* of Isabella d'Este (1497, Louvre,
Paris), besides executing a great many individual paintings. He belatedly
underwent the influence of Giovanni Bellini, his brother-in-law.

ARMION, Simon. French School. Died in 1489. (Page: 104.)—Probably born in Amiens, he became a celebrated miniaturist at Valenciennes, where he is mentioned after 1458. He was in all probability the author of the altar-piece of the Abbey of St. Bertin at Saint-Omer. Influenced by the Flemings, he differs, however, from them by a softness of expression and a simplicity of composition which are typically French. He died at Valenciennes in 1489.

ARTINI, Simone. Italian School. Siena, Died in 1344. (Pages: 29, 30.) —His first signed and dated work is the *Maestà*, a fresco of the great hall of the Public Palace of Siena, whose inspiration and style are akin to Duccio. His style, in turn monumental (*The Condottiere Guidoriccio*, 1328, Public Palace of Siena), or subtly affected (*The Annunciation*, 1333, Florence) asserts itself in the frescoes of the *Story of St. Martin* in the Lower Basilica of Assisi. After 1340, Simone went to Avignon where he painted the since ruined fresco of Notre-Dame des Doms and the Stefaneschi polyptych (Berlin, Antwerp, and Paris). His work in Provence had a great influence on French painting.

ASACCIO. True name TOMASSO DI SER GIOVANNI DI SIMONE DI GUIDI. Italian School. Florence, 1401-1428. (Pages: 34, 36, 40, 44.)—He was formed under Masolino as is evidenced by his early works (*Virgin and St. Anne*, Uffizi, Florence) which have been sometimes ascribed to his master. His friendship with the sculptors Donatello and Ghiberti undoubtedly later contributed greatly to orient him toward the expression of volumes (*The Crucifixion*, Naples). In 1427, he completed the unfinished decorations of Masolino for the Carmine at Florence. In the frescoes of *Adam and Eve*, and in the *Story of St. Peter*, he attains a pathetic quality and a plastic grandeur which considerably influenced the painters of the 15th and even the 16th century.

ASOLINO DA PANICALE. True name TOMMASO DI CRISTIFORO FINI. Italian School. Florence, 1383-1447 (?). (Pages: 35, 36.)—Among his early works are the fragments of an altar picture for St. Mary Major (*Founding of St. Mary of the Snows*, Naples) whose style is very close to that of the choir frescoes of the Collegiata of Castiglione d'Olona where Masolino worked, about 1423-1424. In 1424, after having been accepted into the corporation of painters at Florence, he decorated the Brancacci Chapel at the Carmine, interrupting his work to go to Hungary in 1427. Upon his return, he executed the decorations for the Baptistry of Castiglione d'Olona, in Lombardy. The master of Masaccio, and an artist of elegant grace and pure coloring, he exerted a rather strong influence upon the painters of the first half of the Quattrocento.

ASSYS, Quentin. Flemish School. About 1485/1486-1530. (Pages: 166, 169, 170, 173, 177.)—Born at Louvain, he developed in the environment of Dirk Bouts. About 1491 he settled in Antwerp, where he remained until his death. In 1509 he signed the *Legend of St. Anne* (Brussels). And in 1511 he completed the triptych which had been commissioned three years earlier by the guild of carpenters. Influenced by Italy, he nevertheless retained his Flemish craftsmanship; he was a fine painter of genre pictures (*The Banker and his Wife*, Louvre), and a good portraitist (*A Canon*, Lichtenstein Gallery, Vienna).

MASTER ALFONSO. Spanish School. Second half of the 15th centu (Page: 115, 117.)—He was formerly credited with the altar-piece of monastery of San Cugat: *The Martyrdom of St. Cucufate* (Barcelona) wh was painted in 1473 by an artist named Alfonso. It is known that certain Alfonso of Cordova worked in 1465 at the Royal Palace of Barcelo

MASTER OF THE ANNUNCIATION OF AIX. French School. Mid of the 15th century. (Pages: 97, 101.)—Thus called after the altar-pi of *The Annunciation*, preserved in the church of the Madeleine of Aix Provence. The altar-piece was painted, about 1443, by an artist who l been variously identified with Collantonio, the master of Antonello Messina, with Barthélemy de Clerc, and with Jean Chapus. His wo served as a link between Provence, Burgundy, and Flanders, and considerably influenced the Provençal School.

MASTER BERTRAM. BERTRAM OF MINDEN. German School. Died abo 1415. (Page: 77.)—Born at Minden in Westphalia, he is the oldest kno master working in Hamburg (mentioned in documents from 1379 to 141 His principal work is the *Altar-piece of Grabow* (1379, Hamburg): it conta an important part in polychrome wood, but the artist seems to ha limited himself to painting. His narrative style recalls the Parisi miniatures, but with more naïvety.

MASTER OF THE CŒUR D'AMOUR ÉPRIS. French School. Second h of the 15th century. (Page: 95.)—He was an illustrator for King Re who, himself a painter, liked to surround himself with artists. T miniatures of the *Cœur* (1460-1470) represent one of the high points of t painting of the time by their poetry, their large and clear composition, a the exquisite subtlety of their lighting.

THE MASTER OF FLEMALLE. Flemish School. (Page: 56.)—He h supposedly been identified with Robert Campin of Tournai, the master Jacques Daret and Rogier van der Weyden, born in Valenciennes in 13 and died in 1444. It is supposed also that the works ascribed to the Ma ter of Flemalle may have been painted by Rogier van der Weyden duri his youth. The principal works of this group belong to the Staedel Ir titute of Frankfurt; they were believed to have come from an abbey Flemalle-lez-Liége. Their style resembles that of the Van Eycks ar Weyden, but is more monumental in scope.

MASTER FRANCKE. German School. Mentioned between 1424 and 145 (Pages: 78, 85.)—He worked at Hamburg where he is mentioned betwee 1424-1425. His name is known through the contract of the *Altar-pie of St. Thomas* (December 4, 1424) for a chapel of the church of St. John Hamburg. In addition, two *Pietàs* (Leipzig, Hamburg) and the *Alta piece of St. Barbara* (Helsinki) have been ascribed to him. By its elegan and brilliant coloring, his art goes back to the School of Burgundy.

THE MASTER OF ST. GILES. French School. (Page: 107.)—Probably Flemish origin, for his painting reveals a thorough knowledge of the Fl mish masters, he was active about 1495-1500. The settings of his pictur reproduce with great fidelity the monuments of Paris, a tradition whic seems to have been familiar to the painters of the Royal Domain.

MASTER OF THE LEGEND OF ST. URSULA. Flemish School. Latt half of the 15th century. (Page: 69.)—A miniaturist of Bruges who wa active during the second half of the 15th century. His principal work, *The Legend of St. Ursula* (Convent of the Black Sisters, Bruges), is a diptych in eight scenes which precedes the *Shrine of St. Ursula* by Memlinc.

ASTER OF THE LIFE OF MARY. German School. Known between 1450-1480. (Page: 89.)—Working at Cologne between 1450 and 1480, he came under a strong Flemish influence, especially that of Dirk Bouts. His principal work, *Scenes from the Life of Mary*, is an altar-piece which was offered to the church of St. Ursula at Cologne by Dr. Johann von Schwartz-Hirtz, town councillor of Cologne from 1435 to 1460.

ASTER OF MOULINS. French School. Second half of the 15th century. (Pages: p. 97, 109, 111.)—He has been identified with Jean Perréal or Jean de Paris, with Jean Prévost, a Lyonese artist in stained glass, and more recently with Jean Hay, who has been confused with Jean Clouet the Elder. He was undoubtedly of French origin, even though his art reflects a strong Flemish influence, especially that of Hugo van der Goes. His name is derived from his masterpiece, the triptych of the Cathedral of Moulins, painted about 1498-1499, for the Duke and Duchess of Bourbon. His art, which joins gravity with elegance, has a clarity which is typically French.

ASTER OF THE VERONICA. German School. Beginning of the 15th century. (Page: 82.)—Thus called because of his painting representing St. Veronica (Munich). He was formerly identified with Master Wilhem of Cologne or with Hermann Wynrich of Wesel. He worked at Cologne about 1400; his works are characteristic of the gentle and mystic idealism of the natives of Cologne.

ELENDEZ, Luis. Spanish School. 1716-1780. (Pages: 237, 289.)—The son of a miniaturist, and a painter of still-lifes of great quality, he worked for the castle of Aranjuez. He also painted religious compositions and portraits which foreshadow those of Goya.

EMLINC, Hans (or MEMLING). Flemish School. Died in 1494. (Pages: 59, 66, 69, 70, 97, 166, 167.)—In 1465 Hans Memlinc figures in the directory of the bourgeois of Bruges as a native of Selingenstadt, in the Hessian country of the Rhineland. He undoubtedly developed at Cologne, and then at Brussels under Weyden. Between 1472 and 1491 he worked in Bruges, where he died. His dated works are situated between 1468 and 1491. They show the mark of an exquisite technician whose coloring is brilliant and whose inspiration is full of grace and gentleness (*The Shrine of St. Ursula*, Hospital of St. John, Bruges).

ICHELANGELO, MICHELANGELO BUONARROTTI. Italian School. Florence and Rome, 1475-1564. (Pages: 46, 124, 126, 127, 130, 131, 132, 133, 142, 175, 185, 186, 188, 236, 270.)—Formed at Florence, he worked with Ghirlandaio, and then in the sculpture studio which Lorenzo de Medici maintained in the gardens of St. Mark. Already famous for his *Bacchus* in 1497, he completed the *Pietà* of St. Peter's in 1501 and returned to Florence where he executed for the Seigniory the cartoon of the *Battle of Cascina*. Called to Rome by the Popes, it was not until 1535 that he completed the so-called tragedy of the tombs (tombs of Jules II and the Medici). Meanwhile he worked on the ceiling of the Sistine Chapel, whose decoration he completed with *The Last Judgment*, and he also executed important architectural works (Capitol, St. Peter's). His painting is the prolongation

of his sculpture. It was mainly his *Last Judgment* which profound
influenced the young painters: in its oblique composition and its b
foreshortenings is to be found the essence of the Italian mannerist princip

MORALES, Luis de Morales, called THE DIVINE. Spanish School. Abc
1500-1586. (Page: 225.)—Little is known of his early development.
eclectic painter, he drew his inspiration, in turn, from both the Italia
and the Flemings. He painted numerous pictures of the Pietà, whence l
surname of "The Divine"; he also liked to represent the episodes of t
Passion (*Christ at the Column*, Cathedral of Madrid). He was one of t
great mystic painters of Spain before El Greco and Zurbaran, and he exert
an important influence until the beginning of the 18th century.

MORO, Antonio. Also ANTHONIS MOR VAN DASHORT. Flemish Scho
About 1517-about 1577. (Pages: 174, 184, 267.)—Born in Utrecht,
worked under Jan Schoreel. In 1547, he was enrolled in the guild
Antwerp. Shortly thereafter he left for Italy, and then for Spain (155
1554). In 1553 or 1554 he was in London where he painted the portra
of Mary Tudor (Prado). He sojourned a second time in Spain betwe
1559 and 1560, date of his final return to Utrecht. Truly a Europea
portraitist, Moro left followers in Spain (Sanchez, Coello), Portugal, ai
England.

MORSE, Samuel F. B. American School. 1791-1872. (Page: 305.)—Bo
in Massachusetts, his first artistic interest while at Yale, was miniatu
painting. After study with Washington Allston, he accompanied him
London, coming in contact with artistic and literary lights, eventual
joining Benjamin West's studio. On returning to America, he develope
an individual portrait style. In 1825, he settled in New York, becomir
one of the founders of the National Academy of Design. In 1832, l
invented the telegraph and thereafter gave the major part of his time
science.

MOSER, Lucas. German School. First half of the 15th century. (Pages: 8
86.)—He is known solely through the inscription on the *Altar-pie*
of *St. Magdalen* (Church of Tiefenbronn), dated 1431. He has supposed
been identified with an artist in stained glass of the School of Ulm, ofte
mentioned in the local archives. Interested in perspective and realist
observation, he probably came in contact with Burgundian art, perhaps o
the occasion of the Council of Constance (from 1414 to 1418).

MOSTAERT, Jan. Flemish School. Died in 1549. (Pages: 174, 180.)—H
worked at Haarlem from 1500 to 1505 under the name of Jan Mostersoer
He was painter to Margaret of Austria for eighteen years. In 152
he is known to have been at Malines under the name of Masturt. H
returned later to Haarlem, and died in 1549 at Hoorn. From his *Landscap
of the West Indies*, mentioned in certain documents, and with the aid of
description of one of his portraits, researchers have been able to reconstitut
his lost works.

MULTSCHER, Hans. German School. Ulm, about 1400-1467. (Pages: 8(
88.)—A sculptor and painter of the Bavarian School, born about 1400 a
Reichenhofen, he worked at Ulm as early as 1427, and it was there that b
was reported deceased in a document dated 1467. The *Altar-piece c*

Wurzach was perhaps painted for the hospital of the Holy Spirit in 1437. A rugged painter, Multscher attains a certain grandeur by dint of energy and of an unrelenting observation which does not shrink from ugliness.

URILLO. True name BARTOLOMÉ ESTEBAN. Spanish School. 1617-1682. (Pages: 233, 235.)—He entered the studio of Juan de Castillo in Seville, and later met Velazquez in Madrid. A religious and profane painter, his fame lead him to the presidency of the Academy of Fine Arts in 1660. In addition to his vast compositions for convents (*La Caridad*, 1670-1674), he showed a fondness for themes of the Holy Family: the *Virgin and Child*, and especially the *Immaculate Conception* (Prado). He was also a vigorous painter of popular subjects (*The Beggar Boy*, Louvre).

N

ATTIER, Jean-Marc. French School. 1685-1766. (Page: 258.)—Son of the painter Marc Nattier; academician and professor at the Academy, he was called to Amsterdam in 1715 to paint for the Tsar. He was the portraitist of the Queen and her daughters. His pleasant manner combines the genre portrait with the mythological portrait.

O

LIVER, Isaac. English School. 1556-1617. (Page: 267.)—A miniaturist, born in Rouen, he took refuge in England in 1568, where he was a student of Hilliard. He also traveled to Italy, and his art was deeply marked by his sojourn at Venice in 1596. Oliver's son, Peter (1594-1647), was also a miniaturist.

SONA, Rodrigo de. Spanish School. Mentioned between 1505 and 1513. (Pages: 112, 115.)—School of Valencia. Formed by his father, who bore the same name, the younger Rodrigo continued the elder's work, accentuating the characteristics which tended toward the Italian School (*Adoration of the Magi*, London).

P

ACHER, Michael. German School. About 1435-1498. (Pages: 88, 92.)—Painter and wood-worker, born undoubtedly at Neustift, near Brixen; mentioned after 1467 as a citizen of Bruneck and as the head of an atelier specialized in the making of altar-pieces; he is especially noted for three works: the *Altar-piece of St. Wolfgang* at St. Wolfgang am Abersee, the *Altar-piece of Gries*, and the *Altar-piece of the Fathers of the Church* (1483, Munich). He underwent the influence of Padua and Venice (especially through Mantegna), of the Flemings, and of Multscher. Preoccupied with perspective and grandeur, his highly expressive and powerful art was to exercise a considerable local influence.

AOLO, Giovanni di. Italian School. Siena, 1403 (?)-after 1482. (Page: 42.)—Perhaps a student of Taddeo di Bartolo, later influenced by Fei, Sassetta, and Gentile da Fabriano (*Madonna in a Landscape*, about 1436, Boston). A member of the painters' guild, he was appointed Rector in 1446. His *Scenes from the Life of St. John the Baptist* (Art Institute of Chicago; National Gallery, London), two series of scenes inspired by the same theme, comprise his masterpiece and are an excellent example of his narrative style which develops in vast landscapes whose composition reflects the Florentine perspectivists.

PARMEGIANINO. True name FRANCESCO MAZZOLA. Italian School. Parma, 1503-1540. (Page: 132.)—Born into a family of painters, he was formed by its members, Pier-Ilari and Michele Mazzola. He worked mainly at Parma, at first on the frescoes of San Giovanni Evangelista in 1530 on the frescoes of the Steccata, and from 1533 to 1534 on the Castello di Rocca di Fontanellato. Retired to Casal Maggiore, he went mad before his death. Impressed by Michelangelo at Rome (between 1523 and 1527), he created a particularly refined form of Italian manneris (*The Madonna with the long neck*, Pitti) whose influence was considerable in Italy and France.

PATER, Jean-Baptiste. French School. 1695-1736. (Pages: 248, 251.)—The son of a sculptor from Valenciennes, he was instructed and counselled by Watteau. Imitating his master, he became the painter of the "fêtes galantes" (gay parties or entertainment), but he never attained Watteau inspired beauty.

PATINIR, Joachim. Flemish School. Died in 1524. (Pages: 166, 178, 179.)—Probably born in Bouvines, near Dinant, he was enrolled as master in 1515 at Antwerp, where he died. It was perhaps at Bruges under Gerard David, that he learned the art of landscape. He signed several pictures which serve as a basis for a critical study of his work (*Landscape, with the Flight into Egypt*, Antwerp). His style is close to that of Bosch; and he is deemed the creator of landscape painting in Flanders.

PEALE, Charles Willson. American School. 1741-1827. (Pages: 302, 305, 306.)—Born in Maryland, this artist was a jack-of-all-trades having reputedly engaged in the professions of saddler, coach-maker, taxidermist, silversmith, sculptor and dentist. In 1765, a meeting with Copley in Boston probably influenced his development as an artist. The following year he went to London to study with Benjamin West. Returning to Maryland, he received numerous commissions, including a portrait of Washington at Mount Vernon. In 1776, he removed to Philadelphia, painted, engaged in political and civic projects, taught, founded a museum.

PEALE, Raphaelle. American School. 1791-1872. (Page: 304.)—Born in Annapolis, a son of the celebrated Charles Willson Peale, he studied in Philadelphia with his father. In 1800, he set himself up in this city as a miniaturist. Among the first Americans to paint still-life, he has enjoyed a revival for the modern quality of his work.

PERUGINO, Pietro. True name PIETRO VANNUCCI. Italian School. Perugia, 1446-1524. (Pages: 44, 46, 124.)—Undoubtedly formed by Fiorenzo di Lorenzo, he was a member, as early as 1472, of the Guild of St. Luke at Florence. In 1481, called to Rome, he executed frescoes for the Sistine Chapel, and in 1493 he decorated the convent of St. Mary Magdalen at Florence. Shortly before 1500, Raphael became his pupil and worked with him at the Cambio of Perugia; Perugino considerably marked the beginnings of his illustrious pupil. An art of calm equilibrium which arranges harmonious forms in vast landscapes bathed in a blond light, Perugino's painting, which was popularized by his devotional pictures (*St. Sebastian*, Louvre, Paris), was to lay the foundation of the Umbrian School.

PIAZZETTA, Giovanni Battista. Italian School. Venice, 1683-1754. (Page: 192.)—He studied at Bologna under Giuseppe Maria Crespi, and early underwent the influence of the naturalist currents of Venetian painting at the end of the 17th century. That early manner, which sets colors in contrast, was followed, after 1730, by a clearer coloring of high luminosity (*Ecstasy of St. Francis*, Vicenza). Piazzetta had a great influence upon Tiepolo.

PISANELLO, Antonio. Italian School. Verona, 1397-1455. (Pages: 33, 38.)—Veronese painter and medallist, perhaps the student of Stefano da Verona. In 1431 he completed, in the Lateran, the frescoes of Gentile da Fabriano whose work influenced him a great deal. A court painter, he worked for the Este family at Ferrara and the Gonzague family at Mantua. He decorated several churches of Verona (San Fermo, 1425; San Anastasia, between 1435 and 1438). A portraitist and religious painter, his subtly refined art is the most elegant expression of the Gothic and chivalrous traditions of the Italian courts.

PLEYDENWURFF, Hans. German School. 1420(?)-1472. (Pages: 88, 89.)—Born probably at Bamberg in 1420, settled in Nuremberg in 1457, where he died in 1472. His work has not been sufficiently studied. The following paintings may be attributed to him with certainty: the *Crucifixion* (Munich). Remains from the former *High Altar of the Elisabethenkirche* (Nuremberg and Breslau), where he stayed in 1462. A visit to Cracow in 1470 is mentioned in documents. *Portrait of a White-Haired Priest* (Nuremberg).

POLLAJUOLO. True name ANTONIO BENCI. Florentine School. 1432-1498. (Page: 40.)—Florentine painter, sculptor and goldsmith. He had studied with Ghiberti, Donatello and Paolo Uccello. From 1465 he usually worked with his brother Piero, who was less talented. In 1475 he painted the *Martyrdom of St. Sebastian* (London, National Gallery), a work which soon became famous. His last known painting is the *Coronation of the Virgin*, painted for the Collegiate Church of San Gimignano. As in his sculptures, Antonio the painter had a passion for incisive and sharp lines; Botticelli and Signorelli were deeply influenced by his harsh and nervous style.

PONTORMO. True name JOCOPO CARRUCCI. Italian School. Florence, 1494-1556/1557. (Pages: 132, 133.)—His father, an obscure disciple of Ghirlandaio, was also a painter. Pontormo studied under and collaborated with Andrea del Sarto who influenced him a great deal (works for the Servite Brothers). According to Vasari, Michelangelo's admiration for the arms of Leon X (façade of the Annunziata) caused a misunderstanding between Pontormo and his master. He then elaborated a complicated art under the influence of Dürer. He was at the same time a profane decorator of great charm (Villa di Poggio a Caiano, 1526), a religious painter (*Deposition*, Cappella Capponi, Santa Felicita) and a portraitist of somewhat disturbing insight (*Cosimo the Elder*, Uffizi Florence).

POUSSIN, Nicholas. French School. 1594-1665. (Pages: 147, 238, 23?, 240, 245, 269.)—Born at Villers (Les Andelys). The sojourn of Quentin Varin in Villers seems to have decided Poussin's career. He ran away on foot to Paris where he entered the atelier of George Lalleman and Ferdinand Elle. After a difficult beginning, he went to Rome in 162? where he married the sister of the painter Dughet. Famous, surrounded by a group of attentive disciples, he finally accepted to go to Paris as First Painter to the King. However, soon disgusted with intrigues and frivolity, he returned in November of 1642 to Rome, where he was to remain permanently. The creator of historical painting, he gave more and more importance to landscape and finally made it the actual subject of his pictures. His deliberate, rational art (He wrote: "I have never neglected anything.") is the highest and purest expression of French classicism.

PRATT, Matthew. American School. 1734-1805. (Page: 305.)—Son of a Philadelphia goldsmith, he was apprenticed to his painter-uncle, James Claypole, tried an unsuccessful commercial venture in Jamaica, eventually ended up in Benjamin West's studio in London. In 1768 he returned to the Colonies, settling in Philadelphia, where he was known for his portraits as well as for his decorative signs.

PUCELLE, Jean. French School. About 1330-1340. (Page: 22.)—An illuminator whose art, in the *Breviary of Belleville* (Bibliothèque Nationale, Paris), sets the style of the French miniature for a whole century. If the iconographic motifs and certain architectural details come from Italy, the elegance of the line and the discreet verve of the narration are characteristic of the nascent School of Paris.

Q

QUARTON or CHARONTON, Enguerrand. French School. (Pages: 95, 98, 99.)—A native of the diocese of Laon; undoubtedly formed in a Franco-Flemish environment; his style probably evolved and changed in Provence. He worked in Avignon between 1447 and 1461. There are only two known works ascribed to him: *The Virgin of Mercy* (1452, Chantilly) and the *Coronation of the Virgin* (1453-1454, Hospice of Villeneuve-les-Avignon). With its monumental composition which recalls a sculptured tympanum, the latter work is painted with certain effects worthy of a miniaturist. It is one of the masterpieces of the Provençal School of the 15th century.

R

RAEBURN, Sir Henry. English School. 1756-1823. (Pages: 270, 283.)—Born near Edinburgh in 1756, he studied with a goldsmith, then with the portraitist David Martin, before entering the studio of Reynolds in 1778. He went to Italy and remained two years before returning to establish himself in Edinburgh, where he had a brilliant career. An academician and painter to the King in Scotland in 1822, he was a portraitist full of freshness and vigor.

RAPHAEL, RAFFAELLO SANTI. Italian School. Rome, 1483-1520. (Pages: 36, 122, 124, 125, 126, 129, 132, 143, 185, 233, 238, 270.)—His father, Giovanni Santi, a grain merchant, was also a painter, poet, and sculptor, Raphael probably worked at first under Timoteo Viti, then, in 1499 at Perugia, in the atelier of Perugino. His early Umbrian manner is full of charm and softness (*Vision of a Knight*, London) under the influence of Perugino (*Marriage of the Virgin*, 1504, Brera). Between 1504 and 1508 he was in Florence, developing under the example of the masters of the past as well as Michelangelo and Andrea del Sarto (*La Belle Jardinière*, Louvre). During his sojourn in Florence he also painted several handsome portraits (*The Doni*, Pitti). Called to Rome in 1508 by Jules II, he utilized all his talent in the decoration of the Stanze or private apartments of the Vatican (1508-1515). In addition, he produced tapestry cartoons, decorated the Farnesina, directed the Roman excavations, and continued the construction of St. Peter's. He provided a great inspiration for French classical art, and his last works, interpreted by his pupils, played a large role in the formation of Italian mannerism.

REMBRANDT. REMBRANDT HARMENSZ VAN RIJN. Dutch School. 1606-1669. (Pages: 188, 206, 207, 209, 210, 212, 213, 214, 269, 299.)—Born at Leyden, he was a student of Swanenburch there, about 1623; later he studied for six months under the direction of Pieter Lastman in Amsterdam, where he went to live after 1631. He enjoyed success until 1650, painting for the Stadthouder Frederick Henry, for the town and the corporations of Amsterdam (*The Night Watch*, 1642). The last years of his life were marred by financial troubles, especially after 1654. It was during this period that he painted perhaps his finest works (*The Anatomical Lecture*, 1656; *The Syndics*, 1662). His chiaroscuro permits him to express meditation (*The Philosopher*, Louvre), or even the very soul of his models (*His own Portrait*, Louvre).

RENI, Guido. Italian School. Bologna, 1575-1642. (Pages: 186, 188.)—A student of the Carracci and of the Italianized Fleming, Calvaert, Reni also underwent the influence of Caravaggio (*St. Sebastian*, Louvre) and of classic art, through Greco-Roman works (*Atalanta and Hippomenes*, Naples). His Madonnas were popularized by engravings and copies, and they contributed to spread the vogue for expressive figures in France during the 17th and 18th centuries. That somewhat superficial aspect of Reni's art contrasts with the beautiful portrait of his mother (Bologna).

REYNOLDS, Sir Joshua. English School. 1723-1792. (Pages: 200, 269, 270, 276, 278, 284, 285, 305.)—He began his career in London with Thomas Hudson, and completed his instruction in Italy where he arrived in 1749 to spend three years. Upon his return, he rapidly became famous, and in 1768 he founded the Royal Academy for which he wrote the "Fifteen Speeches." "Every painter," said he, "should seek to attain the Grand Style." That is what he himself attempted to do throughout his considerable production, aided in his studio by numerous collaborators. It is to Reynolds that belongs the merit of having elevated the portrait to the first rank of English painting. His gracefully elegant and aristocratic portraits of women (*Mrs. Siddons*, London) and his children's portraits, painted in a freer vein (*Master Carew*) had a tremendous influence which was further accentuated by his role as theorist.

RIBERA, Jusepe. Spanish School. 1588-1652. (Pages: 223, 226.)—Born near Valencia and studied with Ribalta. While still very young he went to Italy and settled in Naples. He was greatly favored by the intellectual classes. Called "lo Spagnoletto," he made much money and was treated kindly in Italy. His free and masterly technique places him among the great masters of all times. His output was vast and greatly influenced the painting of Spain.

RIGAUD, Hyacinthe. French School. 1659-1743. (Pages: 205, 245, 247.) —After working at Montpellier and Lyons, he won the Prix de Rome, but did not go to Italy. Famous at an early date, he became a member of the Academy in 1687. His success obliged him to surround himself with collaborators. Official portraitist (*Louis XIV*, Louvre), he left magnificent likenesses of the celebrities of his time (*Bossuet*, Louvre).

ROBERTI, Ercole de. Italian School. Florence. Died in 1496. (Page: 47.) —A Ferrarese painter, he underwent the influence of the Bellinis and of Mantegna whom he met either in Padua or in Venice. If one accepts the year 1450 (and not 1456) as his date of birth, it is feasible that he developed by working with Cossa at the Schifinoia Palace of Ferrara. In the service of the Ferrarese court he executed numerous decorative works. A fine colorist and a keen draughtsman, he often attained a great intensity of expression (*Pietà*, National Gallery, London).

ROMNEY, George. English School. 1734-1802. (Page: 270.)—Born in Lancashire, the son of a carpenter, he was apprenticed to a country artist and came to London in 1762. There he painted the *Death of General Wolfe*. After having visited Rome in 1773, he returned to London in 1775, where the Duke of Richmond became one of his first patrons. The most important event in his career was the acquaintance, in 1782, with Lady Hamilton, who inspired him in the most remarkable manner. He was a good colorist, but did not aim at Reynold's richness and depth. He had also a remarkable ability of sketching the forms for his subjects at once.

RUBENS, Peter Paul. Flemish School. 1577-1640. (Pages: 175, 177, 178, 188, 194, 196, 198, 199, 200, 201, 227, 240, 248, 266, 267, 269.)—He was first a student of Tobias Verhaecht, then of Adam Van Noort (1591-1594), and finally of Otto Voenius at Antwerp (1594-1598). In 1600 he left for Italy where he became painter to the Duke of Mantua. He returned to Antwerp in 1608, and the following year was appointed painter to the Archduke Albert, ruler of the Low Countries. In 1610 and 1612 he painted for the cathedral of Antwerp his first two great works: *The Elevation of the Cross* and the *Descent from the Cross*. He directed a renowned studio, surveying and completing the commissions executed by his collaborators and pupils. A councillor to Isabella of Austria, the widow of Albert, he carried out successfully several diplomatic missions to Spain and England between 1628 and 1630. A religious decorator (sketches and compositions for the Jesuits of Antwerp, 1620) as well as a profane decorator (*Medici Gallery*, Louvre, 1622-1625), a portraitist (*Helen Fourment*, Louvre), and a genre painter (*The Kermesse*, Louvre; *The Garden of Love*, Prado), he became a landscape artist at the end of his life. His tremendous work dominates the entire 17th century of Flemish art.

RUISDAEL, Jacob Van. Dutch School. About 1628/1629-1682. (Pages: 212, 221.)—The son of a picture-frame maker, he was also the nephew of Solomon Van Ruysdael who was undoubtedly his master. In 1648 he entered the Guild of St. Lucas at Haarlem, and later obtained the rights of a burgess in Amsterdam, where he lived until 1681. A landscape artist, he drew his inspiration mainly from the wooded dunes and the beaches around Haarlem. His influence was considerable in Holland and France in the 19th century.

S

SARTO, Andrea del. True name ANDREA D'AGNOLO. Italian School. Florence, 1486-1530. (Page: 128.)—He studied under Piero di Cosimo, and his early works show the influence of Da Vinci. Called to the Court of Francis I, he remained in France to paint the canvas *Charity* (Louvre), but returned to Florence the following year. In 1523, he completed the frescoes of the Chiostro dello Scalzo; and in 1525 his *Madonna del Sacco* announced a new style. It was in Sarto's atelier that the mannerist painters Pontormo and Rosso were formed, as well as the painter-historian Vasari.

SCHONGAUER, Martin. German School. Died in 1491. (Pages: 89, 91, 150.)—A painter and engraver, born in Colmar (probably about 1453), the son of an Augsburg goldsmith, he worked in his native city, traveled in the Low Countries, and died at Alt-Breisach, where he had painted frescoes for the cathedral. In painting, his only authenticated work is the *Madonna with the Rosebush* (St. Martin's Church, Colmar) in which he shows the assimilation of Rogier van der Weyden's influence by beautiful, warm tones of red and gold. His reputation as an engraver was great, and spread even to Italy. An admirable technician, he remains Gothic by his predilection for an expressive and decorative line capable of strong accents (*The Bearing of the Cross*) or graceful highlights (*Virgin seated in a Court*), which was to be remembered by Dürer.

SERRA, Pedro. Spanish School. Died in 1379. (Pages: 113, 115.)—The Serra brothers, Jaime and Pedro, worked in Barcelona during the second half of the 14th century. The works of Jaime, the older, are strongly influenced by the Sienese School (*Altar-piece of St. Sepulcro*, Saragossa). Pedro, who painted a great deal in Catalonia, created the type of nursing Virgins in which Italian traits are joined with a fine earthly sense of local color. The influence of the Serra brothers was to be felt during the entire 15th century.

SIGNORELLI, Luca d'Egidio di Luca di Ventura. Italian School. Umbria, about 1440-1523. (Page: 46.)—Formed under Piero della Francesca to whom he owes both the luminous quality and the sense of space of his early works (*Nativity of St. John the Baptist*, Louvre, Paris), he worked first at Cortona, then at Loretto (before 1480), at the Sistine Chapel in Rome, and at Monte-Oliveto Maggiore (1497). His principal work remains the frescoes of the Dome of Orvieto (1499-1506). His powerful style and muscular nudes show his dependence upon certain Florentine masters (Pollaiolo, Verrochio). A figure of exceptional boldness in placid Umbria, Signorelli announces the art of Michelangelo.

SMIBERT, John. American School. 1688-1751. (Pages: 293, 297, 299.)—Born in Edinburgh, the son of a dyer, he worked into art via the professions of house-painter, coach-painter and copyist. Studied in London, spent three years in Italy copying old masters. Sailed to America in 172 at the suggestion of Bishop Berkeley, his best-known sitter. Eventually settled in Boston, enjoying success with the gentry as a portraitist.

SNYDERS, Frans. Flemish School. 1579-1657. (Pages: 174, 201, 203.)—Student of Pieter Brueghel II (in 1593), and of Hendrick Van Balen. A painter of animals and still-lifes, he journeyed to Italy about 1608, and the following year was in Antwerp. He collaborated with his brother-in-law, Cornelis de Vos, as well as with Rubens. His works were highly esteemed in his day: the King of Spain commissioned a large number of them which are preserved at the Prado.

SOEST, Konrad Van. German School. End of the 14th century-beginning of 15th century. (Pages: 80, 85.)—The outstanding representative of the School of Westphalia, he worked during the last ten years of the 14th and the beginning of the 15th century at Dortmund. He undoubtedly sojourned in France, in Burgundy and in the vicinity of Paris (about 1400 and after 1410). His principal works (altar-pieces of Nieder-Wildungen, about 1424(?), and Dortmund) show an inspiration at the once and realistic. He had a great influence on the painting of north-west Germany, between Cologne and Lubeck.

STUART, Gilbert. American School. 1792-1866. (Pages: 298, 305.)—Born in Rhode Island, son of a Scotch snuff grinder, Stuart at 14 studied with the Scottish painter Cosmo Hamilton who, before his death, took him to Edinburgh. He returned to America determined to become a painter. In 1775, he went to London, entered Benjamin West's household for five years. By 1786, Stuart was a leading fashionable painter in London, married and living extravagantly. To escape his debts, he fled to Ireland, thence returning to America in 1793, opening a studio in Philadelphia, at that time the seat of the Government. Here he painted his three Washington portraits and other official likenesses. In 1803, Stuart followed the capital to Washington, D. C. In 1805, he moved to Boston, where he completed his brilliant career.

STUBBS, George. English School. 1724-1806. (Page: 280.)—Born at Liverpool, he was an engraver and painter of enamels. Settled at Leeds, and then at York, his early works were portraits. In 1760 he went to London and became a painter of animals, specializing particularly in the representation of race horses. He is the author of "The Anatomy of the Horse."

SULLY, Thomas. American School. 1783-1872. (Pages: 303, 306.)—Born in England of an actor's family, he was brought to America as a child. After a short training, he set himself up as a miniature and portrait painter. In 1808, he sailed for further study in Europe, was influenced by Sir Thomas Lawrence in London. After two years, he returned to Philadelphia, where he occupied a prominent position and executed a large number of portraits.

'ENIERS, David, called THE YOUNGER. Flemish School. 1610-1690. (Pages: 200, 204.)—A pupil of his father, David Teniers the Elder, he was patronized as early as 1647 by the Archduke Leopold-William. He settled in Brussels where he became Court painter to the Archduke and curator of his collection. Taking his inspiration from Rubens and Brouwer, he adapted genre painting to the taste of his aristocratic clientele.

'ER BORCH, Gerard. Dutch School. 1617-1681. (Pages: 208, 216.)— A student of his father, Gerard Ter Borch the Elder, and between 1632 and 1635 a pupil of Pieter Molyn in Haarlem, he was decisively influenced by Frans Hals. He traveled in England, Italy, Spain, and France. In 1646, at Munster, in Westphalia, he painted his masterpiece: *The Peace of Munster* (London). In addition to painted and engraved portraits, he left numerous scenes of everyday life.

'HEUS, Jeremiah. American School. 1719-1774. (Page: 302.)—Born in Switzerland, he arrived with other members of a German-Swiss colony in Charleston, South Carolina, in 1739. His style suggests both fashionable French and English influences. A successful portraitist, Theus also painted crests, coats-of-arms, coaches, etc., accumulating a considerable fortune as South Carolina's leading painter.

'IEPOLO, Giambattista. Italian School. Venice, 1696-1770. (Pages: 188, 191, 253.)—A student of Lazzarini, he was strongly influenced by Piazzetta, Bencovich, Sebastiano Ricci, and Veronese. Famous at a very early date, he frequently worked outside Venice. A skilful decorator with a wonderful pictorial fantasy (Villa Valmaran, Palazzo Labbia), his clear coloring and his gentle glow serve him well in his religious painting (*Communion of St. Lucy*, Church of the Holy Apostles, Venice) and in his mythological themes (*Triumph of Aphrodite*, Dresden). He worked at the castle of Wurzburg, and, after 1762, went to Spain, where he was to die He was a prodigious draughtsman, and the greatest Italian painter of the 18th century.

TINTORETTO. True name JACOPO ROBUSTI. Italian School. Venice, 1518-1594. (Pages: 140, 142, 227.)—He spent a brief apprenticeship in the atelier of Titian, but also owed a great deal to Bonifazio Veronese, Pordenone, Bordone, and to post-Michelangelesque mannerism. He revealed his talent in the decorations of Santa Maria dell'Orto and in the Scuola di San Rocco (1549-1587). He was prodigiously active, as is shown in his work on the Palace of the Doges (Voting Chamber, Ante-Collegio, Senate, etc.) where he finished, at the age of seventy, the *Paradise* of the Great Council Hall. He also decorated San Giorgio Maggiore with an important series of works. A powerful portraitist, he subordinated the brilliant color of the Venetians to the play of light, thus creating moving compositions with a new and dramatic vision which opened the way to baroque art.

TITIAN. True name TIZIANO VECELLI. Italian School. Venice, 1490-1576. (Pages: 51, 131, 134, 136, 137, 138, 147, 185, 201.)—A student of Giovanni Bellini and also of Giorgione, whose influence is felt in his early works (*Sacred and Profane Love*, Borghese Gallery, Rome), a religious painter (*Assumption*, *Pesaro Madonna*, Frari, Venice), and a mythological painter

(*Bacchanalia*, Prado, Madrid), Titian developed a majestic art of sumptuous coloring. Towards 1540, his treatment became more rapid, his inspiration more moving, and he abandoned himself to searching for colored harmonies in an intermittent light. A penetrating psychologist and an incomparable portraitist, from his first melancholy figures (*Man with the Glove*, Louvre) to the later portraits of *Charles V* (Prado) and *Paul III* (Naples), Titian left a magnificent series of beautiful and radiant works.

TOMMASO DA MODENA. Italian School. Modena, 14th century. (Page 31.)—Born in Modena, the son of a painter, he developed in the environment of the Bolognese miniaturists. In 1352 he signed the frescoes of the Capitulary Room of the Dominicans at Treviso, where he painted the most illustrious representatives of the order with a violent realism. Summoned to Karlstein by Charles IV, he played an important role in the formation of the Czech School.

JOHN TRUMBULL. American School. 1756-1843. (Pages: 300, 305.)—Born at Lebanon, Connecticut, son of the Governor of the State, he was intellectually precocious, entering Harvard at the age of 15. For a while he taught school while attempting to paint. In the Revolution he secured a commission, becoming Washington's aide-de-camp on the strength of his skill as a draughtsman. In 1778, he decided to devote himself entirely to art, making the pilgrimage to London and Benjamin West's studio. Back in America, he painted a series of historical canvases, enjoyed prestige but not fortune. In 1815, he executed some much-criticized murals for the Rotunda in Washington.

TURA, Cosimo. Italian School. Between, 1429-1430 and 1495. (Page : 40.) — He doubtless worked with Mantegna at the Eremitani of Padua between 1452 and 1456 ans likewise passed through Venice, where he must have admired the works of Vivarini and Giovanni d'Alemagna and the frescoes by Andrea del Castagno. From 1457 onwards, he was to work mainly for the Court of Ferrara which entrusted him with the task of painting decorations and numerous portraits He was the founder of the School of Ferrara. Harmonious assimilation of the most diverse influences in a forcelul, dramatic and highly personal style is what distinguishes his work. (Piétà, Louvre.)

U

UCCELLO, Paolo. Italian School. Florence, 1396(?)-1475. (Pages: 36, 43, 46.)—Painter and goldsmith, he collaborated with Ghiberti on the second door of the Baptistry of Florence. Between 1425 and 1432 he was active at Venice, working on St. Mark's Church. His figure on horseback of *John Hawkwood* (Dome of Florence) gives the illusion of sculpture, just as his *Battles* (Uffizi, Louvre, National Gallery), express violence by audacious foreshortenings. The culmination of his scholarly research is found in the *Chiostro verde* of Santa Maria Novella, which he painted between 1440 and 1450. This painter fascinated by scientific certitudes, was also a lyric artist with great warmth of coloring (Altar-piece of Corpus Domini of Urbino, 1455-1458).

VAN CLEVE, Josse. Also JOAS VAN DER BEKE. Flemish School. Died in 1540. (Pages: 85, 177.)—He was long called the Master of the Life of Mary, after the name of his works which are preserved in Munich and Cologne. He lived in Italy, at Genoa, between 1501 and 1506. In 1511, he was enrolled as a master in the corporation of painters of the city of Antwerp. Van Cleve's coloring makes one think of Massys, and the latter's influence is especially marked in his portraits.

VANDERLYN, Pieter. American School. 1682-1778 (?) Page: 299.)—Born in Holland, Vanderlyn emigrated with his compatriots to the Nieuw Amsterdam colony, eventually worked in upper New York State, painting the Patroons of the Hudson River in a style that blends contemporary Dutch and English influences. He also painted signs for inns.

VAN DYCK, Anthony. Flemish School. 1599-1641. (Pages: 188, 198, 200, 205, 240, 267, 270, 271).—A student of the mannerist Van Balen, and a freemaster in 1618, he had at that date already produced several master-pieces (*Drunken Silenus, Crucifixion of St. Peter*, Brussels). He became a collaborator of Rubens, and between 1617 and 1621 his manner is hardly distinguishable from that of his elder. During a sojourn in Italy between 1622 and 1627, he painted several remarkable portraits (*Cardinal Benti-voglio*, Pitti). After a probable journey to Holland (1627-1628), he had 100 portraits from his iconography engraved. In 1632, he was showered with honors and knighted in London, as painter to Charles I. In England he was mainly a brilliant portraitist of the Royal Family (*Charles I*, Louvre) and of English aristocracy (*Lord Wharton*, Hermitage). His influence was preponderant in the formation of the school of English portraitists.

VAN EYCK, Hubert and Jan. Flemish School. First half of 15th century. (Pages: 46, 56, 57, 58, 59, 60, 61, 63, 72, 101, 116, 150, 170, 203.)—Hubert van Eyck is known through the inscription painted on the frame of the *Altar-piece of the Lamb* (Ghent); he died before 1432, for Jan finished the polyptych at that date. He was an artist of repute whose name still appears in various documents. The career of his brother Jan is better known: a court-painter, entrusted with diplomatic missions, he died at Bruges in 1441. By analogy with the polyptych of the Lamb, certain other works are ascribed to Hubert (*The Hours of Turin*, Milan; *The Three Marys at the Tomb*, Van Beunigen Collection, Rotterdam); but there exist ten works by Jan signed and dated between 1432 and 1439 (*The Arnolfini*, 1434, London) to which a certain number of other paintings have been like-ned (*The Virgin of Autun*, Louvre, donation of Chancellor Rolin). The art of the Van Eycks, with its extraordinary technical beauty, joined idealism with a most attentive observation of reality.

VAN DER GOES, Hugo. Flemish School. Died in 1482. (Pages: 59, 71, 72, 107.)—Neither the date nor place of his birth is known. In 1467 he was already considered a master in Ghent, where he worked until 1475, date at which he withdrew to the monastery of the Red Cloister, near Brussels. About 1474-1475, he painted his masterpiece, *The Adoration of the Shepherds* (Uffizi, Florence), a work which was to mark deeply cer-tain Italian painters. At the end of his life, his painting attained a pathetic violence (*Death of the Virgin*), and before his death he went mad.

VAN ORLEY, Bernard. Flemish School. About 1492-1542. (Pages: 174, 176.)—Born in Brussels; son of the painter Valentine Van Orley. Appointed court-painter to Margaret of Austria, ruler of the Low Countries, he worked at Malines between 1518 and 1521. On falling out of favor in 1527 he was again named court-painter in 1532, this time to Mary of Hungary. To his paintings and his portraits should be added a number of tapestries and cartoons for stained glass windows. He was the most outstanding artist in Brussels during the first half of the 16th century.

VAN DER WEYDEN, Rogier. ROGIER DE LA PASTURE. Flemish School. About 1400-1464. (Pages: 56, 62, 63, 64, 66, 71, 85, 88, 89, 91, 99, 105.)—A native of Tournai; the works of his youth have given rise to numerous controversies. He was the student of Robert Campin at Tournai. His first work known to be authentic is the *Descent from the Cross* (Escorial) painted in Brussels where he had just settled (in 1436 he is mentioned as a municipal painter. In 1449-1450 he traveled in Italy, and the Italian influence is perceptible in certain paintings (*Braque Triptych*, Louvre, Paris). At the end of his career he painted the so-called *Bladelin Altarpiece* for the church of Middleburg. He has left numerous portraits. His dramatic style, of vigorous simplicity, imposed itself on the Flemish artists for a whole century, like that of the Van Eycks.

VELAZQUEZ. DON DIEGO RODRIGUEZ DE SILVA. Spanish School. 1599-1660. (Pages: 115, 227, 230, 234, 240, 269, 287, 291.)—Born in Seville; in 1612 he entered the atelier of Francisco Herrera the Elder, and then from 1613 to 1618 he worked under Francisco Pacheco, whose daughter he married. After an initial journey to Madrid, he went to live there definitely. He made two trips to Italy (in 1629, then in 1649), and he made the acquaintance of Rubens in Madrid. Painter to the King, and Marshal of the Court, he received the Cross of the Order of St. James. He began by painting "Bodegones," before attacking religious and mythological subjects (*The Drinkers*, Prado).

VERMEER, Johannes. Dutch School. 1632-1675.—(Pages: 208, 217, 218.) Born at Delft, in a family of modest tradesmen, Vermeer was admitted, in 1653, to the Guild of Saint-Luke in that city. His education remains a closed book: we do not know who was his master or if he went to Italy. Though prized exceedingly by his contemporaries, he was to fall into neglect before his death. Thenceforth, till the 19th century, his name was quoted only by chance. Among his works may be mentioned: *The Serving-Maid with a Jug* and *The Girl with a Glass of Wine*.

VERONESE. True name PAOLO CALIARI. Italian School. Venice, 1528-1588. (Pages: 131, 141, 227.)—This native of Verona was one of the most brilliant representatives of Venetian painting. He was formed by Caroto and Badile, but came under the influence of Parmegianino, Primaticcio, and Brusasorci. He illustrated with great spirit the Venetian festivals which he evoked, under the pretext of sacred themes, in vast architectural arrangements (*Marriage of Cana*, Louvre). Towards 1570 he underwent the influence of Tintoretto and Bassano, and in 1578 he began to decorate the Palace of the Doges (Collegio, Ante-Collegio, Great Council Hall). His tranquil art exerts its charm through a harmony of subtle coloring and a luminous quality unequaled in the Venetian School.

ERROCHIO, Andrea del. True name ANDREA DI CIONE. Italian School. About 1435-1488. (Pages: 40, 44, 48.)—A painter, sculptor, and worker in gold, he had as master the goldsmith Verrochio, whose name he appropriated. Called to Venice in 1483 to execute the Colleone, he was to die in that ci'y.

VIGÉE-LEBRUN, Elizabeth-Louise. French School. 1755-1842. (Page: 263.)—Daughter of the pastellist Vigée, and wife of the art dealer Le Brun, she was painter to the Court of Louis XVI, and especially to Marie-Antoinette and her entourage. In 1790 she emigrated to Italy and traveled throughout Europe, continuing to paint portraits.

VINCI, Leonardo da. Italian School. Florence and Milan. 1452-1519. (Pages: 40, 48, 67, 118, 119, 120, 121, 123, 124, 150, 166, 238.)—Formed in the atelier of Verrochio (1468-1476), he was enrolled in the corporation of St. Luke in 1472. His oldest works are the altar-piece of *The Annunciation* (Louvre), *The Annunciation* of the Uffizi, and the unfinished *Adoration of the Magi* (1481, Uffizi). In 1483 he entered the service of Ludovico the Moor and worked on the equestrian statue of Francis Sforza (1490-1494). From that period date the majority of his architectural projects, and it was then also that he painted the *Virgin of the Rocks* and *The Last Supper* for the refectory of Santa Maria delle Grazie. After the fall of Ludovico the Moor, Da Vinci went from Florence to Milan (1506-1512), and then to Rome. Occupied with scientific work for the Pope, he left unfinished the fresco of the *Battle of Anghiari* for the Great Council Hall in Florence. He painted the *Mona Lisa* and the *Virgin and St. Anne* before leaving for France, where he was called by Francis I, in 1516. He died in France three years later at Cloux, near Amboise. His theoretical work is tremendous; painting and sculpture were for him only steps in a scientific research to which he finally devoted himself entirely.

VIVARINI, ANTONIO DA MURANO. Venetian School. 1435 (?)1476(?).— Venetian painter. Mentioned between 1435 and 1476. Born of a family of painters and mosaicists working in Murano, near Venice, where Byzantine traditions were kept very pure until the 15th century, he worked in Venice, Parenzo, Milan, Padua. He was influenced by Gentile da Fabriano and Pisanello and combined the Northern Gothic style with a hieratic manner, which he drew from Byzantine art.

VOUET, Simon. French School. 1590-1649.—Born in Paris, this young painter reached Venice in 1612. He found inspiration in the works of Veronese, which gave him a taste for vast, well-ordered and rather theatrical decorations. Towards the end of 1613, Vouet betook himself to Rome, where he was to come strongly under the influence of Caravaggio. In 1627, at Louis XIII's behest, Vouet returned to Paris and enjoyed a brilliant reputation until Poussin supplanted him. He died in Paris in 1649. Among his works may be mentioned: *The Presentation in the Temple*, *The Prophet Elias ascending to Heaven* and *Abraham's Sacrifice*.

W

WATTEAU, Antoine. French School. 1684-1721. (Pages: 200, 248, 249, 254, 255, 257, 266, 270.)—Born at Valenciennes, he worked obscurely at first for an art dealer of the Pont-Neuf in Paris. A student of Gillot,

he became a friend of Claude Audran, who gave him free access to th
gardens and the collections of the Luxembourg Palace. Crozat, in turr
revealed to him the beauty of Venetian works. Watteau practised a
types of painting, which he renewed with great talent. The most origina
form that he conceived was the "Fête galante;" he was admitted to th
Academy in 1717, under the title of "Painter of the Fêtes galantes,"
with his *Embarkation for Cythera* (Louvre) of which he was later to giv
a second version (Berlin). These nostalgic evocations are depicted i
dream-like, semi-imaginary landscapes whose delicate figures, drawn from
the master's sketchbook, provide a sort of poetic commentary.

WEST, Benjamin. American School. 1738-1820. (Pages: 295, 302, 305
306.)—Born Chester Co., Pennsylvania, he received some art instructior
in Philadelphia and New York before proceeding to Europe. In 1760
he settled in Rome, acquiring the Neo-Classical manner. In 1763, he
establis ed himself in London, where he was accorded many honors, was
made historical painter to the Court of George III and helped found the
Royal Academy to whose presidency he succeeded. His school in Londor
helped to educate three generations of American painters.

WITZ, Konrad. German School. First half of the 15th century. (Pages
84, 86.)—Born between 1400 and 1410 at Rottweil; mentioned at Base
after 1434; died between 1444 and 1446 (probably in 1445) at Basel or
Geneva. He is noted for a relatively large number of works, the principal
ones being: the *Altar-piece of the Mirror of the Salvation* (about 1435
Basel, Berlin, Dijon); the *Altar-piece of St. Peter* (dated 1444, Geneva)
and the *Altar-piece of the Virgin* (panels at Basel, Nuremberg, and
Strasbourg).

WOLLASTON, John. American School. Active 1749-1767. (Page: 300.)
—Born in England, this artist developed his style under the all-pervasive
influence of Sir Godfrey Kneller. About 1750 he came to America, settling
in Philadelphia. Later he practised in New York and in the South, his
entire activity in the Colonies lasting about seventeen years. Various
distinct mannerisms are connected with his work. He died in England.

Z

ZURBARAN, Francisco de. Spanish School. 1598-1664. (Pages: 188, 222,
223, 227, 232, 233.)—Formed in Seville by Pedro Diaz de Villa Nueva,
the beginning of his career is little known. He worked mainly for the
convents of Seville between 1628 and 1640 (*The cycles of St. Peter Nolasque
and St. Bonaventure*). At the end of his life, under the influence of Murillo,
his sharp sculptural style became softer. This deeply religious painter
(*Monk in Prayer*, London) left pictures of Saints which are full of pagan
grace (*St. Margaret*, London).

9841-11-50. Imp. CRÉTÉ. Corbeil.
Dépôt légal : 4e trimestre 1950.

DATE DUE